COMMENTS FROM

MW01609944

*"After finishing my first ⸛
I knew it would certainly n⸜
always above the creative edge—a dynamic personality
who brings the best out of all his teachers.
He is a true "Educator!"*
Beth Conroy—Belleville East High School

*"Steven's passion and excitement for teaching are evident.
His professionalism and relaxed style will give you insight
into your students, but more importantly, will give you
insight into yourself and how to improve your teaching!
He has a passion for teaching and inspiring educators."*
Christina Frank—Avery Elementary

*"Steven is an awesome instructor! It was great to have
an instructor who actually models the content strategies
consistently in his teaching! I did not dread going to class
because I knew I was going to learn valuable information
relevant to my classroom. I feel refreshed and excited to
implement these new strategies in my classroom this year!"*
Julie Swigonski—Benton Elementary

*"If I were to describe Steven in one word, it would be 'Passion.'
He is passionate about teaching, but more importantly, Steven
is passionate about making sure that his students 'Learn.'
Thank you, Steven, for the Great strategies, techniques,
and inspiration."*
Suzy McDaniel—Carriel Junior High

*"Steven is professional and interesting and made the content
applicable to the classroom. The time flew by because his instruction is
fun and engaging, and the ideas were relevant
and practical to the real classroom. He can change your
whole outlook on student learning!"*
Letha Wilson—Casey Middle School

"When I signed up for Steven's Cooperative Learning and Student Engagement classes, I felt that I knew a lot about both. And yet, with these classes, one is able to experience real Cooperation and Engagement, from a student's perspective, under the leadership of one with true expertise in 'meshing' content with the invaluable social skills needed today."
April Sabolay—Central Jr. High

"It is so refreshing to take courses where the professor is modeling the pedagogy that is being taught. Steven is knowledgeable, highly experienced, and creates a comfortable environment that promotes a lot of collaboration, creativity, and idea-sharing. There are so many applicable strategies, for all learners, that it's hard to describe! Steven's classes should be a prerequisite for all educators. They are by far the most beneficial and interesting classes I've ever taken (and I've taken a lot!). I only wish I had known about them sooner!!"
Rachel Gasawski—Wydown Middle School

"Steven's classes are not what you'd expect from a graduate course, and I have been so happy with the outcome. They are engaging, fast-paced, collaborative, and Valuable. Everything we did had value and meaning!"
Chelsea Hummert—Freeburg Elementary

"I've had many bad experiences with graduate courses in the past 35 years that I've been teaching. Most of them were boring and not practical at all. But that has definitely NOT been the case with this course! I learned a great deal and it has definitely not been boring! Steven was focused (as he should be) on making the course PRACTICAL! He asked us what we wanted to get out of the course and then provided it. It has been the most useful graduate course I've ever taken, and I have a Master's plus 24! Thank you, Steven!"
David Fahrner—Althoff High School (Science)

ENGAGING THE STUDENT BRAIN

7 Hard-to-Ignore Teaching Techniques That Make Things Stick

by Steven Northup

Copyright 2024 Steven Northup. All Rights reserved. No part of this book may be reprinted or reproduced or utilized in any form or by any electronic, mechanical, or other means, now known or here after invented, including photocopying and recording, or in any information storage or retrieval system, without permission in writing from the publishers. Library of Congress cataloging-in-publication data. A catalog record for this title has been requested.

MRN Educational Limited
Belleville, IL
EngagingEducatorsToday.com
StevenNorthup.com

ISBN: 979-8-9891400-0-8 (paperback)
ISBN: 979-8-9891400-1-5 (e-book)
ISBN: 979-8-9891400-2-2 (audiobook)

Book design and production by www.AuthorSuccess.com

For Andy and Justine, Jesse and Alex,
Sawyer, Charlotte, Jude, Remy, and Violet,
who amaze, delight, and educate me on a daily basis,
and who constantly remind me
that the good life is built on family.

For Becky who brings peace, love, and encouragement
to everyone in her life, every day.

For all my teacher friends, and teachers everywhere,
for the miracles that you perform
every day in your classrooms.
You are magical.

A special thanks to Sawyer for helping with website design,
to Jesse for his editing, and to Andy for his art.

CONTENTS

Hello, and welcome, my friend. I'm Steven Northup, and I believe you have come to the right place at the right time, and that you're about to find answers that have eluded you for years.

Here's my thumbnail— I've been a public school teacher for 35 years, and taught teachers at the graduate level for over a decade. I've also had a lifelong curiosity about the brain, and an unquenchable desire to learn the secrets of captivating communication, and the mysteries of human behavior.

So, in a nutshell, you and I are going to simply combine the *art of teaching* with the *science of people.*

This is the buried treasure that holds the power to transform your classroom. Helping teachers is my mission, and I can't wait for you to have this.

Sign up now at www.engagingeducatorstoday.com to get fresh and free 1-Minute engagement tips.

Now, let's get started and have a little fun!

SOFTWARE STRUGGLES

Teachers work all day to change the brain
but haven't been trained to run its software.

HAVE YOU EVER been forced to switch software at school? With little or no training? Not fun.

In the blink of an eye, your years-in-the-making system changes, and you start over. You knew the old program inside out. You had a rhythm and a flow that was fast and efficient. Then suddenly you were completely rug-pulled.

Now you're trapped in a circular maze with glitches that take 20 clicks instead of 2. *"I'm trying to figure this out, but there's just no rhythm. It makes no sense. It's overwhelming and I can't believe this is happening!"*

First-year teachers, like me in '81, expect those kinds of learning curves. But learning how the brain's software works—that's a lot more complicated.

Our entire career focuses on changing the brain,
and we simply haven't been trained.

But teachers are survivors. And with time, most figure out bits and pieces that make life easier. Still, we definitely aren't neurologists. We don't understand the brain. There's just too much information. It's way too complicated, mumbo jumbo magic. And brain scientists speak an alien language.

During my first year of teaching, I became fascinated with finding the secrets of this mystery—how to talk to the brain. *"I am going to figure out the* rhythm *of this thing."* (I'm also a musician.)

Then it became a hobby—a game. When I learned something new, I would do a live experiment the next day with my kids. And Bingo! Things started working in my classes.

Gradually, with more university degrees and studies, plus endless independent research, my fascination continued to grow. I kept learning, experimenting, and practicing. Then, other leadership offers started popping up.

"Hmm . . . This stuff works across the board. Not just in the classroom."

Later, I was hired to teach graduate-level classes specifically designed for working teachers. Our class dynamic was that of a facilitator and team, and we always learned a great deal from each other. Priceless.

More leadership opportunities, speaking engagements, and professional development (PD) requests followed and honed my skill sets—especially the PDs. You and I both know how teachers feel about those.

True story—I was once asked to do a district-wide, 2-hour PD workshop. After school. On a Friday. The day before

Christmas break. Without a net. Talk about a *student engagement* challenge! But against all odds, we had a blast, and they left encouraged with some great new tools.

Here's My Point . . .

I'm a lifelong teacher and learner whose mission, for many years, has been to help teachers. And my goal today is to offer you the best, most practical value available on this topic. Because what you do is amazing, and the world needs you now more than ever!

So . . . how will this book work for you? What's different about it? And what's in it for you?

It works like this . . .

It's Simple and Practical

This is a Quick-read. No fluff. No BS. You will learn to partner with your students' human nature and teach in rhythm with their brains. Their resistance will relax, learning will improve, stress will drop, and fun will return.

Your Personal Trainer

This career classroom teacher, and master teacher instructor, will blend brain instincts with best practices into a personal training session for you.

My Promise for You

This book doesn't just talk about teaching; it *teaches* teaching. Everything is modeled for you so that you can experience it personally, as a student. Skeptical? No problem.

What's different about this book?

You are about to learn the secret recipes for teaching in rhythm with the brain and human nature. But you won't learn a bunch of formulas—you will *experience* everything in person. Your brain will *feel* the *"aha . . ."* That's how you will know this is real.

That's how this book is different. It fills gaps you didn't know you had. I'll show you right now . . .

(*Below is a super-quick lesson that models techniques that are in rhythm with you. Stay aware of your emotions and thoughts, and notice the "aha" at the end. Starting now . . .*)

This is our SAMPLE CONTENT:

The brain runs on a few fundamental principles that can't be broken. We can either use them for good, or fight them and fail.

Here's the lesson . . .

Stop and think about a riveting novel that completely immersed you in the story. Spellbinding. It pulled you in and you became Involved. It felt real. You could see it. Hours flew by.

"I can't put it down!"

(Remember how much you love that feeling?)

"I do. But how did the author create that magic?"

Answer: That book partnered with your human nature. It worked *in rhythm* with your brain's natural instincts and principles. That's what created that *magical music in your mind.* It's like a secret recipe.

Now, think about a book you were excited about but completely discarded within minutes. Why?

Because it ignored the principles that the brain looks for and has to have. That's why it failed. Even though it may have been technically well-written, it didn't use the secret recipes. And you could quickly tell that it had no rhythm. It quickly turned your brain off, and that was the end of engagement.

When our teaching methods violate, or ignore the instincts of the brain, learning suffers.

(*End of modeling . . .*) Did you *feel* the *"Aha . . .?"*

What's in it for you?

Here's a snippet of what you will learn:

- Why students ignore teachers, and how to be Un-Ignorable.
- What's important to students (and it's not what you think).

- How to make their brain your ally instead of your enemy.
- Fun ways to improve student focus.
- How to reduce resistance and raise motivation.
- Ideas, strategies, and techniques you can use in class tomorrow.
- New perspectives and ideas that are missing in education today.

FINDING YOUR RHYTHM

Did you know that Einstein was a musician too, and that he credits the *music in his mind* for his greatest discoveries?

My mission is to show you these natural *rhythms* of the brain, and have you experience them personally. Then, as you begin to understand this *music of the mind*, you'll start to feel its drumbeat and naturally begin to teach in rhythm.

It will feel even better than the old software you knew inside out. When you find the *brain's* rhythm, you'll never look back. Your students will also feel the difference right away, and they will want to be your partner. Your teaching will naturally lead their dance and bring out the best in each one.

The Map of the Book

Each chapter will do the following:

- Give the big-picture snapshot right up front and summarize the key points later. You can't miss them; they will be easy to re-find later.

- Simplify and clarify the concepts with unique analogies, graphics, insights, evidence, and stories, allowing you to feel each strategy personally and know that it works.
- Overflow with strategies and techniques to use tomorrow.
- Be valuable, meaningful, and important to you.
- Build on, and align with, every other chapter.
- Highlight Brain Breaks throughout to allow your brain to relax and refresh.

Part 1 will show you how to easily recognize the simple drum beat and rhythm of the brain. You will feel a natural connection and ease in understanding its nature.

Part 2 will show you the secret principles and recipes so that you can naturally teach and recreate that same rhythm and dance with your students.

Part 3 will be application.

So, my friend, it's time to stop doing the robot. We both know it's not working.

Instead, let's partner with our students' nature and start teaching in rhythm with the instincts of the brain. It's a lot more effective and fun for everyone.

PART ONE
BRAIN MAGIC REVEALED

WHAT DO YOU DO when your kids don't understand? Because they weren't listening.What can you do? Do you say it again? Slower? Louder?

——When I tell people that I'm color-blind, they invariably
start speaking slower and louder,
"Can you see *This* color!?"
Color-blind, not deaf.
People are funny.——

Or do you try saying it in a different way?
But what if you are still met with a blank stare and it feels
like you are speaking different languages?

Trying to communicate in
different languages isn't great.

I'm learning Spanish and thought I was doing pretty well until I decided to try it out at a Mexican restaurant. I was greeted by a friendly man at the front desk whose English was as small as my Spanish. It got comical pretty quickly.

Things fell apart when I asked if they allowed indoor dining (during the pandemic). He didn't understand, and I defaulted to the pantomime hand motion thing.

My Spanish practice session didn't go quite as well as I had imagined it might, and this is exactly what happens in our classrooms every day. We expect a communication gap, but never in the way it plays out in reality.

With different languages, we expect a barrier, but with the same language, we falsely assume that we are communicating effectively.

So, what can we do in our classroom, when Rachel understands a concept and Sara still doesn't, even after using every trick we know? Obviously, we're not speaking the *language* of Sara's brain. Let's call that *Saranian*. (wink)

Here's a simple, yet powerful, Hard-to-Ignore teaching technique for you.

———— Especially effective with teenagers. ————

USE A TRANSLATOR

"Rachel, do you understand what I'm saying?"

"Sure."

"Tell her what I mean."

"Okay."

10 seconds later Sara understood completely.

Here's more good news—translators can also work in reverse when *we* don't understand what the *student* is thinking. Sometimes I felt clueless trying to understand Sara's logic and reasoning.

I've also had the same feeling when trying to understand a toddler's unique language. My two-year-old grandson was chattering away a mile-a-minute, teaching me how to play with his toys, when he realized I was not getting it. After repeating things 23 times even faster didn't work, he even tried holding my face in his hands and speaking in slow motion.

"Fwee, I'm faying Fwee! Fffffwwwweeeee . . .!"

After my 37th fail his patience ran out and frustration took over. He threw his hands up and stomped off to tell his mother . . . (*"Chatter . . . Chatter . . . Chatter!"*)

About that time, his four-year-old sister walked in, put her hand on her hip, and said, *"He wants you to be the sheep."*

That little lesson taught me to start saying, "Rachel, what does Sara mean?"

10 seconds later I understood completely.

Sara was also very patient with my lack of understanding of Saranian.

Bonus Tips

- Watch and learn what Rachel does differently, and why she is so effective. (i.e. Fwee = sheep)
- Try using this technique sooner rather than later to save a lot of time and frustration (like my grandson).
- Think of it as working smarter and delegating to a native speaker of *Saranian*. It not only helps to save our sanity, but it also protects Sara's self-esteem and our relationship overall.

80/20 RULE

HAVE YOU HEARD of the 80/20 Pareto principle? It states that for many outcomes, roughly 80 % of results come from 20 percent of causes. In other words, 20 % of our strategies and efforts create 80 % of our results.

Natural wisdom would then advise us to double down on the most effective 20 % in order to reap the best return on our investment of time and effort.

So, instead of focusing on learning just Saranian, let's learn a bunch of simple ways to speak the *universal* language that engages, and speaks to, (almost) *all brains*.

We'll call it—(wait for it)—Albranian. (Smile)

The pages above model the following **Hard-to-Ignore teaching techniques**.

- *Puns and corny humor communicate comfort and safety in Albrainian* (speaks to all brains, it's universal).
- *Weird Words are engaging, memorable, and fun* in Albrainian.
- *Building commonalities, showing cool vulnerability, and admitting mistakes creates connection, relation-ship, and safety in* Albrainian.

Can you find them?

Keep studying our pedagogy, my friend. Notice *your* emotions and level of engagement. Let's keep going and have some fun along the way.

RESEARCH?

WHO'S WRONG?

Science or Experience?

Biology or Psychology?

With debates like these, *Balance is best.*

When choosing "research" to rely on, I have the mindset of a hard-core investigative reporter; very skeptical. I'm just like you—just a few steps ahead.

There are, however, some proven facts about the brain that are known to be biologically true and unchanging. Knowing how to use these basic facts is an absolute necessity for teachers.

Teachers desperately need to partner with human nature.

And always keep in mind that Balance is Best.

Evidence-driven wisdom and real-world understanding are far more valuable than debatable theories.

Like this little story . . .

The Lion

Lion, Weasel, and Fox decide to hunt rabbits together for the day. At the end of the day, Lion tells Weasel to divide the sizable pile of rabbits evenly. Weasel does. Lion is furious and swallows Weasel in a flash. He then tells Fox to divide the rabbits evenly. Fox takes the single smallest rabbit for himself and leaves the rest. With a rumbling voice Lion says, "How did you learn to count so well?" "I learned from Weasel."

Moral of the Story—Fox survived because he quickly learned to partner with Lion's *nature*. We will also succeed when we learn to partner with our students' *human nature*.

Brain Break / Refresh

KEY POINTS: Remember these **Brain Facts**

1. The *Way* the brain thinks and learns doesn't change and is driven by *Instinct*.
2. *What* the brain thinks and learns, constantly changes, sometimes quickly, and is driven mostly by *Emotions*.
3. *Why* the brain chooses to think about and learn something, is driven by *Importance*. (i.e. Survival/Needs)

Grasp and hold onto those Key Points, my friend.

They are *Very Important.*

"When our teaching methods violate, or ignore the instincts of the brain—learning suffers."

Let's change that now.

When we don't understand the instincts of the brain, we can't know when our teaching methods violate, or ignore them.

Many traditional methods do violate, and we are completely unaware. For example, we know that boring things put people to sleep. *But we don't realize that it's the brain's survival instinct to conserve vital energy in action.*

Teachers work all day to change the brain but haven't been trained to run its software.

My goal is to train you to use the software so efficiently that you naturally begin teaching in rhythm with the brain.

When you find the *brain's* rhythm, you'll never look back, and your kids will look at you in a whole new way.

When we change the way we look at people, people change the way they look at us.

A Promise to You

I will skip the science-speak and excessive explanations.

Everything we do together will have a purpose and will model our principles and techniques for you.

So, challenge yourself to keep looking for the teaching techniques and methods that are effective for *you*, as the student. Many will be pointed out, but just like real teaching, many will be invisible. So, stay sharp and watch for the hidden clues.

Like right now, the promises I just made have a very intentional purpose. If they helped *you* personally feel one step more engaged, motivated, and connected, then it has been effective, and you should consider using something similar for your kids. Tell them what you are doing and why. *Keep showing the Compelling Benefits for them personally.* Promise yourself.

All of this is Albrainian (all brains). Using things that are *Instinctively Important* to *you*, my student, is the secret to engaging the brain. And also *telling you* (key!) that that is our intentional goal. It speaks to all brains. It's universal.

With these promises, the teacher has now become accountable to you, the student. That's Albrainian. *All brains innately understand the weight and importance of statements like these.* It is powerful for the students and the teacher.

This is how to build a partnership and how excellent education happens. So, just like I'm *telling you* now, *tell your students*.

You just felt it. You know it works.

As you read, be aware of how your emotions shift. With new ideas and answers, you may feel just a little lighter. It may feel energizing as *your* mind and imagination are engaged and your motivation grows. It might start to feel kind of *fun* to think differently and to feel a little creative again. You may even feel empowered as you discover some answers that you have sought for so long.

All of this is by design. Take our model and let it motivate you to do the same for your kids. You're experiencing it now, in our first few pages together.

Let's keep going, my friend, and figure out how to engage our students' minds in the same fun ways.

BEHIND THE CURTAIN

Now it's time for us to take a quick look behind the curtain to see how the magic happens.

We know it's a teacher's job to create magic in the minds of our students. The problem is that most teachers have never been taught the hidden principles of the mind to make that happen. As a result, we repeatedly do things the hard way, like a magician without the secret. So watch very closely, and be kind of *Sherlocky* as we begin to change that right now.

(Psst . . . did you catch that little magic trick?)

The trick itself was very sleight-of-hand and easy to miss. Did you notice what happened in your mind when you read *Sherlocky*?

Think about it. In hindsight, are you able to realize how it felt and how it sparked your engagement for a few invisible seconds? Can you see how it instantly conveyed the concept and context, in the blink of an eye? That was the magic.

And here's the secret to making that magic happen . . .

Weird/Made-up Words are engaging, can explain complex concepts instantly, and are highly memorable.

Remember this— *Weird Words are Wonderful!*

Like Sherlocky. Or Albrainian. (All brains, it's universal.)

And now that you know the *secret*, you can use
that magic wand tomorrow and forever.

That's how we teach in Albrainian.

It works. You just felt it.

Brain Break/Refresh . . .

BONUS SECRETS !

*Add a simple hand movement to the Weird Word, and that
concept will become Un-Forgetable!*

EVEN BETTER - Enlist the kids to help create, and teach
these things, and they will remember it FOREVER!

(Smiles)

A Present for You . . .

Great Ideas are great.

But too many, too fast, can be too much.

So how about a new 1-Minute Quick-Tip, straight to your
inbox, once a week?

I know there are a ton of ideas here, and it can feel overwhelming. That's why I have a couple of gifts for you, to
help ease the burden.

1. Sign up for our newsletter and get a free Quick-Tips each week, that you can use that day, and practice for the week.

   Kind of like an auto-pilot improvement routine Small steps, regular repetition, and no planning.

2. And as a welcome gift, for joining our tribe, you'll get our most-requested guide for free:

**FROM APATHY to AMBITION—
The Top 3 Brain Secrets to
Motivate Lazy Learners**

**Sign-Up Now at EngagingEducatorsToday.com!
Subscribe Here!**

It's always a privilege, never taken lightly, to be invited to your email. We promise to only send the good stuff!

PS . . . BETTER THAN CHOCOLATE AND WINE!

Please take 2 seconds to review the book here! (link text)

It's more important to our success and survival than chocolate and wine!

(Seriously—It really IS a huge favor you could offer!) Thank you!

HOCUS FOCUS

Student Focus Techniques

Improving our students' focus is one of those impossible magic tricks we all want to pull off. But, again, we are trying to make brain magic while ignoring human nature and unbreakable brain instincts. Why do we do that? Because . . .

Teachers work all day to change the brain but haven't been trained to run its software.

Let's begin to change that right now. We are going to give you a guided tour behind the curtain and reveal the secrets for you.

The "Secrets Behind the Magic"
are coming so. . .
(buckle up!)

To improve a student's focus, we first need to get their attention.

1. **A Hook**. Something to grab attention. Something that grabs their *focus* and holds on tight.

2. **Tell them**, *"Wow, you were really focused for a minute there."* Push them to see that they can and did focus. Their brain immediately starts analyzing, "What? Huh? What do you mean? Hmmm . . . that's weird!"

3. **Ask them**, *"What did that focus feel like? What caused it? Curiosity? Humor? Fear? Confusion?"*

4. **Tell them**, *"Whatever caused it was Important to you and* made *you focus for a minute."* Explain that they automatically focused because that hook was Important, in some way, to their brain, and was Un-Ignorable.

5. **Show them** that *they can* practice and improve their focus whenever they want by using this same pattern themselves.

It's the same pattern you and I have used together from the beginning. A corny joke, weird word, or unique story piqued your interest. Then you learned the techniques that were used to engage your focus.

That caused you to realize, and want to analyze your own engagement, and how you could use that strategy with your students. It could be a new twist on an old idea. It could be a new concept altogether. Or maybe just knowing how, and *Why* it works.

When you *felt* it work personally, in your mind, it became *Instinctively Important* for you. You naturally focused internally to figure out this new and interesting experience.

Now, when you start using this same pattern consistently with your class, your kids will also start looking for the invisible *Moral of the Story*. And that will grow their focus in fun ways. Like these next examples (more modeling coming up).

FOCUS ON PHYSIQUE

Did you know that your muscles can only pull? They can't push. The muscles in our body can only contract; they can't push. It's true. Look it up. *(This is step 1 our Hook.)*

Now that you are thinking about your body, let's use that interest to improve your focus. *(This is step 2, Making You Aware.)*

We know that kids are oblivious to just about everything. The world around them, the people around them, their **vocal volume**, etc. They are also oblivious to their bodies and their thoughts. They're oblivious to everything. They haven't yet learned to focus, that's for sure. *(Step 3)*

One way we can get them to think about something magical and invisible like focus is by using their physical body. By using mindfulness techniques or yoga stretches or even simple calisthenics, we can introduce them to an awareness and inner focus on the feeling in their muscles. *(Step 4)*

If you've never done anything like this before, you could use the following script as a pattern for lots of different activities. *If you are a veteran, you won't need the script, but be sure to study the beginning and end. They are Important.* (*Step 5*)

"Okay everyone, I'd like for you to stand up straight and face forward. We are going to try something weird."

("weird" makes it *Instinctively Important* and intriguing in Albrainian. Now they're listening.)

"We are going to do a little experiment to see if we can feel something invisible." ("feel" and "invisible" = intriguing)

"It will take 60 seconds, and I will do it too."

(Teacher too = Importance.)

"But you will have to be quiet and concentrate, or you may miss it." ("...you may miss it" builds more curiosity)

(All of this was step 1, The Hook.)

STRETCH POINT (Activity)

Say this calmly and slowly:

Stand up straight. Feet shoulder width apart.

Keeping your right arm straight, point to the wall in front of you.

Now, without moving your feet, twist to the left as far as you can.

Carefully watch where your finger is pointing, and mark the farthest spot on the wall with your eyes. Memorize the spot.

Now, come back to center, face forward, and relax.

Shake out your arms. Do a couple of arm circles.

Next, we are going to repeat the same thing, but this time, stretch a few inches farther, memorize where your finger points, and see if you can feel an invisible difference inside your body and where you feel it. Ready?

Wait! Follow these directions. Straight right arm pointing forward, feet solid, and twist as far as you possibly can . . .

a little more . . . hold it there . . .

mark the spot with your eyes . . .

and come back.

Shake out your arms. Do a couple of arm circles.

                    Take a slow, deep breath in, then out.

Wow! I could see that your mind was much more focused the second time. (step 2)

Think about this. Did you feel something invisible inside your body? Which muscles did you feel stretching the most?

In a whisper, like a secret, tell your partner what you felt in your muscles and what was surprising for you. (step 3)

> ("whisper", "secret", and "surprising for you"
> are energizing and engaging in Albrainian.)

Now I have a question for you. Since you went as far as you could the first time, how were you able to go farther the second time? What do you think? What did you feel in your muscles? Whisper with your partner again.

Now explain that they were actually practicing and improving their focus, along with stretching. They focused hard on stretching their muscles farther, and also on the spot on the wall. Their improved thinking (focus) was a big part of their success.

Moral of the Story . . .

Tell them why their brain focused so well. (step 4)

- It was a Goldilocks Challenge. (juuust right)
- It was completely personal.
- Their stretching muscles woke their emotions.
- These things are all *Instinctively Important* in Albrainian.

The brain automatically focuses when we do Instinctively Important (personal) things. It won't ignore them. It's Un-ignorable.

Now, Always Remember to Finish the Lesson, my friend!

Don't leave the job half-done! (a most common mistake)

Ask, *"Do you think you could do this by yourself? Whenever you want? Could you practice and improve your focus a tiny bit more each time?"*

Tell them, *"The answer is yes. One reason you stretched farther the second time, was that your focus had improved a little bit. Your brain was a little smarter already!*

We are going to keep practicing this, from time to time, because better focus is one of the most important things we can learn. When our focus gets better, we listen better, we learn more, people like us more, and we make more money."

(This is step 5) Get them to buy in with things that are *Important* to them. We have to *Sell* things like 'Personal Best' and 'Education' if we want them to *buy in*.

Teachers tend to leave out this critical piece of the puzzle. (Another most common mistake)

You get the idea.

You can do this in a million different ways.

Here's another . . .

SQUARE BREATHING

Square Breathing is another great way to practice awareness and focus. Like this: *"Eyes closed, breathing slowly and deeply, inhale deeply four counts . . . hold four counts . . . exhale completely four counts . . . hold four counts. Repeat a few times."*

Use the same five steps and scripted questions to guide their thoughts.

LIFESAVING TRIVIA . . .

When our breathing slows and deepens, it signals to the brain that we are safe. *It turns off the fire alarm.* (And teachers *Love* that moment!) But the opposite is also true, and creates more stress and anxiety, and sends the brain into Lock-Down. Zero learning happens in Lock-Down.

Slow, deep breathing triggers the brain to lower blood pressure, heart rate, *fight or flight* stress hormones, and to feel safe again. Its door unlocks and opens to learning. In this simple way, by intentionally slowing our breathing, we can change our emotional state in a matter of minutes.

Square Breathing is also an excellent tool for teachers to calm *their* minds and quickly decompress. Every little bit helps. Balance is essential to survive and thrive in teaching.

HERE'S WHAT WE'RE LEARNING . . .

KEY POINTS

- What's the Most Important and engaging thing in the world for kids? Themselves.

- Stopping the world for 60 seconds to *focus* on invisible things that they can feel personally, within their body, in real-time, is a good way to introduce focus and awareness. With quality repetition and practice, the brain's focus will improve.

- Don't forget to take the time to explain all the things we are talking about to your students. Just like the tiny secrets that were revealed for you in parenthesis, tell them these *secrets of brain magic*. If you enjoy learning the secrets, you can know that they will, too. And they will respect you for sharing with them.

Here's another completely different way to practice focus in a fun way . . .

MIXED-UP READING

This is weird but interesting.

Only creative minds can read this. *(wink)*

Cna yuo raed tihs? fi yuo cna wow! The oerdr of the ltteres in a wrod dno't mtaetr. Olny tihng taht mtaetrs is the fisrt and lsat ltteers. The rset can be msesed aonurd. It dseno't mtaetr. The huamn biran deos not raed ervey lteter. It raeds the wrod adn isntnalty un-srcabmels tehm. Azanmig huh? And mom awlyas siad slpeling was ipmorantt!

*(**Moral of the story:** Right now you are thinking about your thinking and your focus is improving. It's Albrainian. Un-Ignorable.)*

One more quick and crazy one . . .

BINOCULARS

Tell your students to create make-believe binoculars with their hands, bring them to their eyes, and focus on the Mixed Up Reading again. Try it now for yourself.

"Wow! It's so much clearer!"

(**Moral of the story:** *Focus immediately improves when distractions are removed. It's Albrainian. You just felt it. Tell them and show them.*)

KEY POINTS for Improving Focus

- Show, Don't Tell.
- Don't talk about it, *Be* about it.
- Model it. Practice it. Repeat.

All of the above examples and activities were chosen because they required students to "Do it." They actually *Did* focus and get better in seconds. Their focus was stronger and their results improved instantly.

With each activity, they personally *felt* their focus improve in surprising ways. That's how to create Importance for them. That's Albrainian.

ALERTALERT***ALERT***

PAY ATTENTION!!! YOU ARE ABOUT TO RUIN EVERYTHING WE'VE JUST LEARNED!!!

Pay Attention Right Now: Here come more MASTER KEYS! Without them, the vault will slam shut, and none of this will work or matter. This is where so many teachers drop the ball and come up short. We don't *finish the lesson*. We don't fill in the invisible knowledge gaps and our students miss the most important points. Tell them, tell them, tell them.

Keep showing all the compelling benefits for them.

> ## MASTER KEYS!
>
> - We Must draw their attention to the fact that *they Did Focus*.
> - We must remind them that *they Did It* and *Felt It*.
> - And we absolutely *Must* make them aware, and show them that *their personal focus Improved* in a matter of seconds, with just a tiny bit of practice.
> - Finally—We must use these Master Keys repeatedly. We must consistently show them their improvements and successes, even small ones, that came as a result of good strategies and good effort. Not accident. Not luck. Not even just good effort.

Good strategies make all the difference in how much we improve.

No matter how long or how hard we run east looking for the sunset, it will never happen.
Poor strategy guarantees failure.

Learning to focus does take practice and repetition. If we want something to happen in our classroom, we have to teach it, model it, practice it, and *Sell* it, specifically and consistently.

A young Kindergarten teacher was tired of her class not lining up well, so she decided to make some changes. Then one day, at the end of recess, her class lined up perfectly. A colleague was amazed, *"How did you get them to do that?!"*

"I taught them. And we practiced."

"How many times?"

"Only 4 . . .thousand."

You just experienced the 5 steps again with this *Alert* section. *(Smiles)*

Are you still being Sherlocky and finding the secrets? What was the hook? (step 1)

> *We are what we do repeatedly.*
> *Excellence, then, is not a singular act, but a habit.*
> *Aristotle*

Brain Break / Refresh

MYTH BUSTER

The brain's ability is *Not* fixed, locked down, or preset. It changes constantly, and we can direct and improve its abilities, focus, and wisdom.

We can get better, and learn almost anything, with work and good strategies.

Everything you and I do here, in our short time together, models and practices good strategies and principles that partner with the brain and with human nature. Use them.

And Teach them to your students.

Teach them to your students.

Teach them to your students.

They will love you for it.

PART TWO
THE 7 SECRETS

The Most Important Mindset

What is Communication?

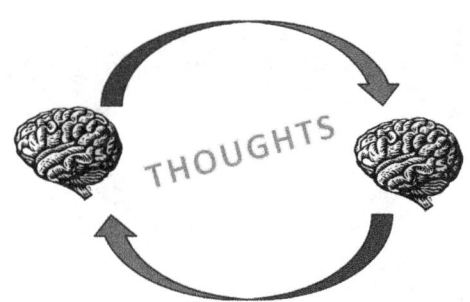

What Hinders Communication?

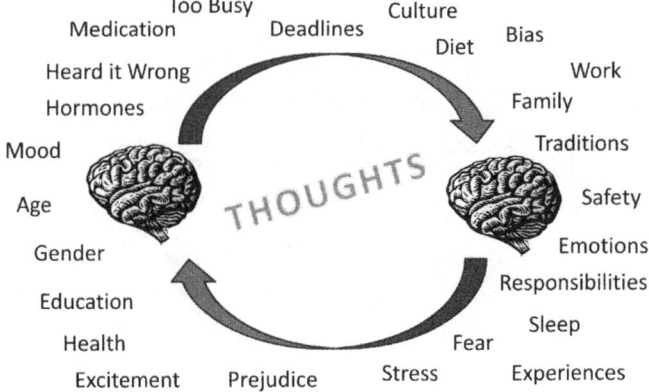

What Hinders Communication?

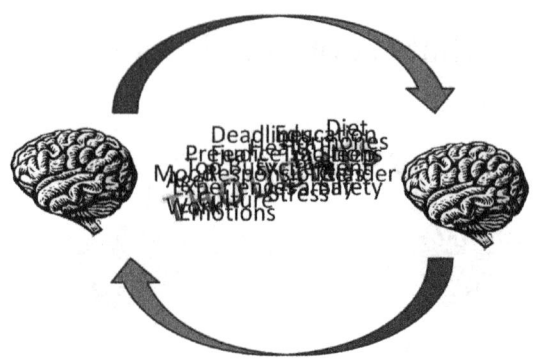

What "Cuts Through" the distractions?

MORE MAGIC REVEALED!

There are certain hard and fast hidden principles (*secrets*) that the brain lives by, including its #1 principle.

#1 SECRET PRINCIPLE of the Brain:
IMPORTANCE DRIVES EVERYTHING

VIP PASS REQUIRED

Play with me for a minute, just for fun. Let's pretend that you went to Vegas and your debt at the casino skyrocketed until 2 huge men in black pulled you away from the table and into a back room. *(Wink)*

"Sign over your house or else, Joey."

"Please, just let me talk to the boss. We're best friends. Just tell him that I'm here."

"The boss doesn't see anything or anybody."

Things are about to get very ugly.

"Wait! Wait! Look at this!"

You pull out a signed picture of you and the boss:

"To my best friend Joey. VIP Pass-Unlimited Access."

How valuable would that VIP Pass be? Let's get one for you right now. *(Smiles)*

Here's the moral of my corny little story.

*KEY POINT—*The brain is the boss, and doesn't see anything or anybody, except VIPs.*

IMPORTANCE DRIVES EVERYTHING

*** This is **the most important** fact to remember about the brain. It is biological, undeniable, and cannot be changed or ignored. This is absolutely the #1 instinct that we must embrace in our teaching methods. Period. **Importance Drives Everything.** ***

When our teaching methods violate, or ignore the instincts of the brain—learning suffers.

"Why do students ignore teachers?"

HERE'S THE HARD TRUTH:

Students ignore teachers because what they say and do
is simply Not *Instinctively Important to them.*

Like Charlie Brown's teacher.

"Wah, wah, waaahhh . . ."

Let's change that right now.

Teaching in rhythm with the instincts of the brain

will make you **Un-Ignorable**.

"But how do I do that?"

Be *Instinctively Important*— Not just Entertaining.

Just like that book you couldn't put down.

Entertaining eventually bores the brain.

Instinctively Important never does.

It is in rhythm with the brain.

Instinctively Important is Albrainian.

Brain Break/Refresh

Mnemonic Mnoment . . .

Remember this—When it comes to Engaging the Brain . . .

Weird is Wonderful!   Normal is Naught!

Mnemonics are simple memory boosters that increase retention 10x in seconds. Acronyms, alliteration and rhyme are classic examples. *Weird words are wonderful! Normal is Naught!* - uses the mnemonic device of alliteration.

Whenever we hear or read alliteration, it engages our brain and makes us slow down and think. Why? Because it's kind of weird.

Regardless if you love it or hate it, it works every time.

It engages the brain, even if you don't like it.

Alliteration is also a Pattern Break.

(i.e. Something that snaps us out of a brain-dead trance.)

All of this with 1 sprinkle of weirdness.

Now, let's create a little *weirdness* to help us remember our #1, most important concept of being ***Instinctively Important.*** 2 big "I" words.

I - I . What weird way could we use I - I ?

Let's do this... From now on, Every time you read ***Instinctively Important,*** say, "I -I Captain!" out loud. (Spongebob Reference)

It's weird, silly, corny fun (even if you roll your eyes), and repetitive. All of which are engaging and memorable. But, adding your voice also incorporates physicality, which innately signals *Huge Importance* to the brain, and sky-rockets retention and comprehension.

All these things are **Instinctively Important!** Albrainian.

("I–I Captain!")

Saying it out loud takes 2 seconds. I'm going to ask you to play along 12 times for a total of 24 seconds of effort. The reward?

The most valuable and important concept will likely be encoded into long-term memory.

And weeks from now, when your class is drifting off, your mind will flash back to **Instinctively Important**, ("I–I Captain!"), and your favorite techniques from this book will pop into your mind.

And that will continue to grow throughout the rest of your career.

Not bad for 24 seconds of silly talk!

Weird is Wonderful!   Normal is Naught!

Ok, brain break's over . . .

IMPORTANCE (VIP)

THE BRAIN INSTANTANEOUSLY rates and ranks everything by its level of *Importance*. Every single thing. Instantly, all at once. By *Importance*. Rustling leaves. Distant voices. Colors. Faint smells. Emotions. Pain. Pulse. Breath. Antibodies. Every thought. Every blink. Every movement. Every. Single. Thing. It ranks everything instantly, by its level of *Importance*. Its mechanism is called the Reticular Activating System (RAS). The brain says:

"Oh great, one more thing to think about! Will I ever get a break? Okay, okay, how important is it really? I'm already overwhelmed. Pumping the heart, counting white blood cells, constantly changing hormones and diapers. 'Mom, Mom, Mom . . .' Do I really need to take on one more thing right now, or can I just ignore it?"

Most of the time, the brain responds the same way you and I do. Ignore it. Or at best, *"I'll get to it later."*

What percentage of the time do we ignore stuff that just isn't Important enough? What do you think? 90% of the time? More?

That's exactly what the brain does. If it's not *pretty Important*, it won't wait 5 seconds before letting it go, to be washed away forever by the whitewater rapids of media in our minds. We both know it's true.

Importance is like the VIP Pass that gets our foot in the door to the brain. Remember: *The boss (brain) doesn't see anything or anybody except VIPs.*

Instinctively Important is the #1 engagement principle of the brain and memory. ("I–I Captain!")

As teachers, it is the #1 main thing that we need to focus on in our teaching, if we want them to listen. And we both know . . . *If they're not listening, they're not learning.*

STOP! WAIT! IT'S A TRAP!!

"What?"

Listen. I know you think you know all of that! You think that you are making lessons important to your kids. But you can do so much better. You just don't know how . . . yet. *You are doing your best,* and you get bits and pieces right, but there is so much more, and better, that you don't know. So *don't sleep on this point!*

Learning to make things **Instinctively IMPORTANT** to their brain is our *KEYSTONE principle!* ("I–I Captain!")

"Okay, Okay! I'm listening! But how can I know what's important to someone else? How do we find their VIPs?"

That is an extremely complicated question with nearly unlimited psychological variations and justifications. But . . .

Einstein praised smart people who make complex things seem simple.

So, in honor of Einstein, here is my simplistic answer:

We know it's a VIP when *they want it.*

If they *want* it then it's **I**mportant to them in some way, on some level. And that means we can use that VIP, that *priority,* to engage and influence their desire to learn.

"But how, when the only thing they want is video games and social media?"

Let's begin by looking at the brain's *Platinum* VIP Pass that is **Instinctively Important**. ("I–I Captain!")

(Can you guess?)

THE MIND AND EMOTIONS

DID YOU KNOW that we make most decisions based on our unconscious emotions (our gut feelings) and *then* rationalize them with logic and reasoning?

According to Harvard scientist Gerald Zaltman (and many others), decisions are generated in the brain's emotional center. He has shown that patients with damage to their emotional centers become unable to make decisions. So, while people may claim that they decide things with logic and reasoning, emotion actually drives most of our decision-making. Not logic.

(That means choosing to learn is an emotional decision.)

We also remember emotional experiences much more so than the unemotional.

Why do we remember our first kiss so long ago but forget where we put our phone?

Why do we remember our favorite meal last month, and forget yesterday's lunch?

An emotional experience during one of the most difficult periods of my life, helped me comprehend the incredible power that emotions have on our minds and memory.

SHE REMEMBERED

Her tortured mind had forgotten nearly everything, including her son, but she remembered one thing.

Alzheimer's is a horrible disease. Good times are rare, but also create vivid memories. When my son came to visit, a strange little miracle happened. Her mind and memory cleared for a short time, and her banter and laughter returned.

"Bend down here and give me a hug you bad boy!"

"I don't think I can bend down that far, Grandma."

"Boy, you better watch out! You know dynamite comes in small packages! I can still turn you over my knee young man!"

She had always been 5 ft of laughing, dancing dynamite.

"What's that mess all over your face?"

"That's my beard! Isn't it cool?"

"It looks terrible! I think a good scrub brush would take care of that in a hurry!"

At a time when few memories remained, she still knew and loved her grandson, and he brought her back for a brief miracle. I'll never forget it.

But that moment was quickly gone and things slowly worsened. When the doctor said the end was near, our days and nights blended and time stopped. Until that late night when she had one last lesson for me to keep. As I held her hand and sat close, I said, "Mom, do you know who I am?"

Confusion, then deep concentration, furrowed her brow. She stared and stared into my eyes . . . and tried to raise her head to lean closer. Then, with the deepest sigh ever, she said,

"No . . . but I know you love me."

> *"People may forget what you said, but they will always remember how you made them feel."*
> —Maya Angelou

This is how incredibly important and powerful emotions can be in our minds and memories.

Now, let's learn how to use that power to improve our teaching.

SURVIVAL

#2 SECRET PRINCIPLE of the Brain:

SURVIVAL FIRST

Survival is the number one job of the brain. Nothing is more *Instinctively Important.* Period. ("I–I Captain!") When the brain feels threatened, it shuts down tasks and processes and diverts all of its resources to its fight, flight, or freeze defenses.

Survival is job #1.

Remember, *Importance Drives Everything*, and nothing is more *Instinctively Important* than Survival. ("I–I Captain!")

What that means for teachers is that **zero learning occurs** when the brain feels threatened. Period. Too much stress, anxiety, fear, and the *school* goes into *Lock-Down*.

Survival First becomes the only thought in the brain.

Rattlesnake!

Imagine peacefully walking through the woods in late autumn.

Calm.   Serene.   Relaxing.

Beautiful colors and sunshine . . .

Suddenly, you step on a stick with dried leaves

and your brain snaps to *"Rattlesnake!"*

Your *'startled cat'* instinct triggers—*"Eeeeek!"*

3 feet straight up!

As you land and see the stick,

your heart attack begins to subside.

That's your brain's *Survival Instinct* in action.
Instantaneous. Unstoppable. Powerful.

Survival is the brain's top job. Period.

*Protect Thy*self is its number 1, most *Important*, priority.

We can't avoid it, ignore it, or change it. The best we can do is understand it and work in rhythm with it.

This also means that *if* something is *essential* to the brain's *survival*, it **will not be ignored.**

***Emotions are essential for survival
and will not be ignored.****

You and I still remember the details of September 11.

LIFE-CHANGING TRIVIA...

CONFUSION IS A GOOD THING.
It means you are about to learn something **new**.

When we Google search something, and the cursor spins,
Google is *Confused*. Our brain is kind of like that.

When we are confused, our brain is searching,
connecting, and creating new meanings.
Confusion = Learning.

A kid says, "I'm never confused, and don't make mistakes.
I'm too smart!"
Nope, sorry. That really means you aren't
learning and growing much.

Tell your kids!

CONFUSION IS A GOOD THING!
It means you are about to learn something **new**.

That's how to teach Growth Mindset.

One caveat: Too much confusion, for too long, feels overwhelming and hopeless. Find *Balance* in all things, my friend. Strive for Goldilocks Confusion—Juuust Right.

EMOTIONS IN EDUCATION

#3 SECRET PRINCIPLE of the Brain:

EMOTIONS ARE ESSENTIAL AND UN-IGNORABLE.

You and I already know from personal experience, that our brain has feelings and opinions about almost everything. But always remember that it is *hardwired* to listen to those gut instincts in order to survive. Studies have even shown that our intuitions can reach 90% accuracy with practice.

(Usher, Marius, Russo, 2011)

Emotions are Instinctively Important to the brain for Survival. ("I–I Captain!")
(Principles 1 & 2—Importance and Survival First)

Remember this:

We make most decisions based on subconscious emotions (our gut feelings), then justify them with logic and reasoning.

However, it's also true that our words can quickly influence and change emotions. Have you ever said a single word that instantly changed someone's emotions?

Man, I have.

HERE'S WHAT WE ARE LEARNING

- Emotions are *Instinctively Important* to the brain. They are like a Platinum VIP Pass that always grabs attention.

- Emotions are highly *engaging* and highly *memorable*.

- Through our words and actions, we create either positive or negative emotions with our students. Constantly. Choose positive.

- Connecting curricular content with *emotions* is a highly engaging and highly memorable teaching tool.

WORDS CHANGE EMOTIONS

The more we can trigger and connect our students' emotions (gut feelings) with learning, the more memorable and Important our words and lessons become for them.

The more we can *show* someone, through our words and actions, that we understand and *get them*, the more they will instinctively begin to trust, value, and listen to us.

For example, *She Remembered* personally showed you *(through the movie in your mind)* how quickly the right words can create powerful emotions, and how memorable they can be. That was our content goal in that moment. 99% of that story *showed* you, and only the quote at the end *told* you.

The specific techniques that were used are *coming soon*, but for now, here's another bite-sized, Hard-to-Ignore teaching technique that can trigger positive emotions within your students in an instant. One small word at a time.

USE HER WORDS

Let's pretend that you know Sara really likes cats and loves to call them "kitty." Okay. So what? It's understood that you could talk to her about cats to build rapport, right?

Of course. But she is also offering us the exact ace in the hole that we have been looking for, and we are completely missing it. Talking about a cat with her is fine, but using "kitty" instead would light up her *emotions*.

Consider this. You hire a real estate agent to find a new house and tell him that you like a very *clean* style. He describes the first house as "beautiful" and he loves it. It turns out to be very ornate, not "clean."

Next house—"This one is stellar-one of my favorites."

Nope. Very traditional, etc.

You keep explaining, he never gets it, and he's fired because there is no connection.

New agent. This guy hears your hidden clues.

First house, he says, "This house has a crisp, clean style."

. . . Hmmm, it seems like he gets me.

And bingo, he got it right the first time. This house lights you up and it's love at first sight.

That's also what "kitty" does for Sara. You think it's minor and silly, but it feels just as important to her.

She won't know why, but she'll *feel* that you understand her when no one else does.   We've both been there.

Use Her Words is a simple technique that can also be used to connect emotion and content.

And let me be clear, we are not talking about memorizing the *Urban Dictionary*. It's simply a bite-sized first step to incorporating the Platinum VIP Pass of *Emotion*. Think of it as the teacher-to-student form of using the right Love Language. It's their Learning Language, and it creates visible motivation instantly.

By stacking a few of these simple tools, you will become fluent in Albrainian and naturally increase engagement, retention, and fun in your classroom.
You will find your rhythm.

You will also begin to see your students' attitudes change from "So what?!" to "Me too!" You are experiencing it yourself. When I talk about how teachers think, the voice in your head shouts, "Me too! That's how I feel!"

*KEY POINTS

- If we want people to listen, we must

Say Important Stuff and Eliminate the Fluff.

- Emotions are like a Platinum VIP Pass in Albrainian. Use them to engage and be Un-Ignorable.
- Favorite words quickly create emotions that increase engagement, retention, and fun in your classroom.
- BOTTOM LINE: When we submit by *Using Her Words* instead of ours, it:

1. Proves we care.

2. Engages her emotions.

3. Forces *our* brain to analyze her *weird* words for an extra half second, which automatically builds more understanding of her point of view. (The 2nd realtor listened and got it right the first time, which translated into money in his pocket.) Not bad for a half-second effort!

SIDE NOTE—This entire book is intentionally written using your words; your Learning Language. That's one piece of the invisible magic that helps us connect, and you are feeling those effects personally.

> Invisible things matter and accumulate, my friend. This is the magical music and rhythm of the brain. ***It's not nothing.*** So, be aware of these benefits, trust your intuition, and use them.

"Intuitions are not to be ignored, Watson. They represent data processed too fast for the conscious mind to comprehend."
—Sherlock Holmes (Wink)

WARNINGWARNING***

OPINION PIECE AHEAD!!!

I believe that trying to sterilize learning by removing emotion and treating it like computer programming is one of the biggest failures in education. The human brain is not a computer. We cannot simply download more and more data and expect it to stick. Yet we continue, then wonder why students lack motivation. That's not how the brain is built. Emotions are essential and are potentially our most powerful tool in teaching.

> *The mind is not a vessel to be filled,*
> *but a fire to be ignited.*
> *—Plutarch (115 AD)*

Teachers know these things are true, but *executives* pressure us to comply, to the point of exhaustion and complacency.

Real learning happens when each unique brain finds its own way to create important meaning out of new information.

> *Real learning takes a lot of energy,*
> *and the brain refuses to just waste it*
> *on irrelevant data being dumped in.*

Conserving energy is another survival mechanism in the brain that cannot be changed.

*KEY POINTS:

- The brain is the boss, and doesn't see anything or anybody except VIPs.
  Principle #1—***Importance Drives Everything***

- Simply put, if new learning is deemed Un-*Important*, the brain refuses to waste its vital energy on it.
  Principle #2—***Survival First***

- *Emotions* are *Instinctively Important* for survival. ("I–I Captain!") That's why they open the door to learning like a *Platinum VIP* pass, and cannot be ignored.
  Principle #3—***Emotions are Essential and Un-Ignorable***

SUMMARY

The more we intentionally elicit and trigger student emotion and connect it with our content, the more Important, Engaging, Motivating, and Memorable it becomes.

The more we connect positive student emotions with our presence, our classroom, and with learning, the more engaged and motivated they will be.

"But how?"

The answers are coming up. Stay tuned! *(Wink)*

Brain Break / Refresh

NEWS FLASH

"New Structure" Discovered in the Brain (2023)

Since I promised to skip all the science-speak, here's the short version. *My slightly impatient paraphrasing:*

Nico Dosenbach, a neurologist at Washington University School of Medicine, and his team have identified a previously unknown structure in the brain that objectively shows the brain and body to be linked.

(Which simply validates what history's greatest minds, including Aristotle and Descartes, have known for thousands of years)

WHO'S IN CHARGE—BRAIN OR BODY?

Both.

#4 SECRET PRINCIPLE of the Brain:

MIND & BODY ARE LINKED.

CHANGING ONE, CHANGES THE OTHER.

The body and the mind are inextricably connected. They can't be separated. Their influence on one another can't be ignored, denied, or turned off. They are 2 sides of the same coin. If the coin gets flipped, both sides spin.

When the body exercises, it tells the brain to release dopamine and endorphins that make the mind feel happy.

When the brain feels fear, it changes the body physically by increasing blood pressure, heart rate, breathing, and blood flow to the limbs, making it easier to run or punch. It also releases cortisol and adrenaline, directing the body into high alert—fight or flight.

Mind & Body are linked. Changing one, changes the other.

Our Emotions are connected in a similar way with our Opinions and Attitudes. We've both experienced this:

"When I have to, it's so hard.
But when I want to, it's so easy!"

Negative emotions create negative opinions and attitudes.

"X is boring."

"Worthless."

"Do I have to?"

Result = *"X is so hard!"*

Positive emotions create positive opinions and attitudes.

"X is fun!

"Exciting!

"Mysterious!"

"I want to"

Result = *"X is so easy!"*

- Emotions change constantly and are easily influenced.
- Opinions last and are very stubborn.
- Trying to change someone's mindset (opinions) is difficult at best.

So how can we use this in our teaching?

CHANGE THEIR MOOD, NOT THEIR MIND

It's hard to change someone's opinion, but we can influence and change their mood for the better. And when done consistently,

Their emotions can change their opinions and attitudes.

When we change their mood, they will change their mind.

We make most decisions based on subconscious thoughts and emotions, (our gut). Remember?

Students care most about how things make them *feel.* They also want to know, *"What's In It For Me?"*

Nearly everything they do is based on their feelings and on bargaining.

*This is a **big deal** for teachers to understand and use.*

Connecting *Good Emotions* and *Compelling Benefits* with our Content makes learning more meaningful, memorable, successful, and fun.

Again, that's how we *partner with* human nature. That's how we teach in rhythm with the brain.

That's Albrainian.

LEARNING NEW STUFF FEELS GOOD

Progress feels good. To everyone. It's Albrainian.

Progress feels fulfilling in our souls.

"Ah man! I'm getting better! That stinks!"
—said no one ever.

Successful learning is *Instinctively Important* in all human brains. It is essential for survival—and all brains instinctively know it. It is Albrainian. ("I–I Captain!")

When we feel like a failure as a learner, a deep sense of fear fills us. *"I can't learn, and my future does not look good."*

But when we connect good emotions with little learning successes, students begin to think they *can,* and their negative self-talk flips. *"Hey, maybe I can . . ."* Remember—

"When I have to, it's so hard.
But when I want to, it's so easy!"

Kids naturally want to learn and feel smarter. All Brains Do (for survival). But when they think they can't, fear fills their belly and stops them dead in their tracks. Fear might look like fear, or it might show up as anger or shutting down.

Logic and reasoning are not likely to overcome those types of fear. Good emotions can. Small victories do.

Over time.

CHANGE THEIR MOOD (about learning), NOT THEIR MIND.

****When we change their mood,
they will change their mind.****

"Okay, sounds great. But how?"

This entire book is filled with great ideas

for you to use tomorrow.

(Stay tuned and stay sharp!)

CREATE CURIOSITY

#5 SECRET PRINCIPLE of the Brain:

CURIOSITY IS THE SIMPLEST MOTIVATOR

Curiosity is another one of our most powerful, and yet easiest engagement tools. It is Magnetic. Un-Ignorable. Necessary for survival. Human nature. Primal. Fun and Exciting. And it can change moods.

Caveat—First and foremost, the curiosity we create must be Important to the students (principle #1) in order to be effective.

Second, if we also encourage their emotions (principle #3) *by being playful*, their curiosity becomes irresistible. These things are both simple and instant when we know how.

"Okay, okay. But I need some usable how-tos for tomorrow."

Yep. Here you go . . .

CLIFFHANGERS!

LET'S KICKSTART YOUR BRAIN by calling this concept *Cliffhangers*. It's not a perfect definition, but it's a start.

What pops into your mind when we say *Cliffhangers*?

"The thing we hate most at the end of the season?"

Yep. Kind of.

Curiosity is very engaging and easy to do.

"But how often could we use something like that in class? Wouldn't it get old pretty quickly? Plus, wouldn't it turn some kids off and cause them to shut down?"

(These questions are tiny Cliffhangers . . . modeling how to Create Curiosity.)

The term Cliffhanger is close, but not complete. Yes, we could use a big season finale type of mystery or unanswered question in our classroom, but we are really talking about the overall idea of *Creating Curiosity* by building a Setup and a Payoff.

Or, we could call it:

- Tension and Release
- Question and Answer
- Dissonance and Resolution
- Or my favorite—Itch and Scratch

Every Itch needs a good Scratch. Every Setup needs a Payoff. Every Question wants an Answer.

PRO TIP:

The Question **has** to be *strong enough* to make the Answer worth the effort (i.e., it has to be *Important enough* to do the work).

Our *Itch/Scratch* or *Tension/Release* method offers a lot more uses for our classroom than an actual Cliffhanger. We can use this method constantly, to great effect.

And by the way, we have been modeling it since the beginning. Remember, everything we do together is modeling and has a purpose. Every question we pose creates an itch. So does every internal question that we create inside of you.

Right now you have lots of questions. That's good. If you are intrigued, we have *created curiosity;* that's the *Itch* or *Tension* that wants answers. It Engages your imagination.

MOSQUITOES?   Invisible Itches

Okay, think with me for a minute.

Something as simple as the title *She Remembered* is like a miniature cliffhanger. It is kind of a *Setup* that asks a couple of questions.

Can you see subtle *Itches* you want to *Scratch*? Little *Setups* that yearn for a *Payoff*? Answers that we *anticipate* discovering? Curiosity is triggered, just a bit. Invisibly. But how?

How is the title *She Remembered,* like a cliffhanger?

(What questions come to mind?)

She Remembered asks . . .

1. *Who* remembered?

2. *What* did she remember?

Get the idea?

In hindsight, can you feel the tiny Itch? Like *mosquito bites*? See the subliminal Setup? Now, after reading the story, you know those answers. This means you received the payoffs—and they were better than expected.

Pro Tip: Always *Over-Deliver* on the Payoff!

We'll look at more examples in a minute, *(that's an Itch)* but when we do, remember to look for the secret behind the magic. Keep asking yourself, "How was the Itch created?" And also, "Why is it Itchy?"

How are the instincts, or rhythms of the brain, being tapped into?

CLIFFHANGER EXAMPLES:

(From previous pages)

"How can we change their mood?"   *Itch*

Create Curiosity and Cliffhangers.   *Scratch*

"BRAIN MAGIC REVEALED"   *Big Itch*

This entire book   *Big Scratch*

How to speak Saranian?   *Itch*

"Use A Translator"   *Scratch*

If you would like more practice and examples, the previous pages are filled with practical models. You will find a Cliffhanger at the end of most pages, with answers on the following page.

Many more classroom examples and techniques coming soon.

(insert commercial break here . . .—smiles)

Let's click the 'refresh button' in your brain, because your brain needs to check out for a minute in order to 'refresh.'   (Modeling again)

Ok, here's my commercial —

Sign-up Now for our Free Newsletter! and you'll receive simple-to-use "5-Star" 1-minute tips, techniques, and activities for Tomorrow! Don't miss a single issue! Subscribe Now! And as a **FREE BONUS** — you will get our most-requested Guide:

FROM APATHY to AMBITION—
The Top 3 Brain Secrets to
Motivate Lazy Learners

Sign-Up Now at EngagingEducatorsToday.com!
Subscribe Here!

It is always a privilege, and never taken lightly, to be invited to your email. And we promise to only send the good stuff.

BETTER THAN CHOCOLATE AND WINE!

PS . . . Please take a second to review the book here! (link text)

It's more important to our success and survival than chocolate and wine!

(Seriously—It really IS a huge favor you could offer!) Thank you!

Okay, back to work!

Your Brain is an Energy Hog.

It is 2% of your body mass, but burns 25% of your energy, **at rest**! Paying attention is hard work for the brain and burns a lot of energy, *especially when we don't care about it.*

The brain can only sustain focus for a short period of time. When it tires, it **will** disengage and *daydream*, to take a break, and conserve energy.

It *always* strives to conserve energy. This cannot be changed. It is a built-in survival mechanism that automatically kicks in, and can't be overridden or stopped.
                              - The Art of Impossible - Steven Kotler

Our attention will ebb and flow naturally. So, let's use that rhythm, and make the brain our ally, not our enemy. Like we are doing... right now.

KEY POINTS: *Cliffhangers*

- *****We can fight against the immutable biology of the brain and lose, or we can dance with it and win. If we don't work *with* it, it will actively work *against* us by ignoring and disrespecting us.

- Cliffhangers partner with biology by creating tension, then release.

- Too much tension, or for too long, and the brain will shut down.

- Not enough tension will be ignored and bored (*"It's not worth the energy"*).

- But when it's *just right* (Goldilocks), it creates a mild, invisible *itch* (engagement) for a short time, followed by some relief (*scratch . . . ahhhh*). This aligns with, and uses, the brain's natural rhythm; its ebb and flow between focus and daydreaming.

This is how we feel the drumbeat and 'dance' in rhythm with the brain!

Teaching Techniques Being Used Right Now:

- We began teaching Cliffhangers with bullet point clues.

- The examples that followed encouraged you to discover the patterns (more on Discovery later).

- These Clues and Patterns allowed you the freedom to create your own *personal meaning* of Cliffhangers (instead of spoon-feeding).

- We then quickly filled in the gaps with the Key Points you may have missed.

- Next, your brain automatically added those new Key Points to your personal meaning, and voila!

- You *discovered* the concept and created your very own original recipe chicken (oops) meaning.

- Your brain worked pretty hard and spent a lot of energy on that task. That effort and work signaled to your brain that the info was *Important*! And since *you* did the work, your brain will keep it; a huge Comprehension and Retention boost. Pretty Cool!

PIXAR?

> Pixar writer/director Andrew Stanton believes in making the audience put things together for themselves. Instead of giving them 4, give them 2 + 2 instead. Audiences actually want to work for their meal—but, without knowing that they're working. That's what makes a great storyteller—hiding the work, which the audience craves, and needs, in order to be engaged and involved.

We accomplish that by leaving small gaps, that the brain can't resist filling.

Andrew is so rich and successful because he speaks Albrainian fluently. Our brains agree with him completely. They are designed to deduce and problem-solve in order to survive, and they enjoy nothing more than discovering the answer.

Rice Krispies—*"Snap Crackle . . . ?"*

Bounty—*"The quicker . . . ?"*

M&Ms—*"Melts in your . . . ?"*

Skittles—*"Taste the . . . ?"*

See? Irresistible. Like a magnet.

A lot more fun and engaging than being spoon-fed truckloads of data. (Boring . . .)

(psst . . . that was another sample of ways to use leading questions in class tomorrow.) Be creative my friend. (Wink)

"The great thing, then, in all education is to make our nervous system our ally instead of our enemy." —William James, 1892

ALLIES NOT ENEMIES

#6 SECRET PRINCIPLE of the Brain:

CREATE LEARNING ALLIES, NOT ENEMIES

HERDING CATS

WE HAVE BEEN TALKING about aligning our teaching with human nature and the instincts of the brain. But, what does that mean? What does it look like? Feel like? How is that possible?

How can we make their brain our ally, not our enemy?

Let's see if we can find those answers in the following simile.

It's been said that teaching is like herding cats.

Hmm . . . Maybe more like trying to *train* them. (Wink)

Step one is getting the cat's attention. But the more you approach, and the harder you try, the more they walk away.

So, *how can we make their brain our ally?*

By using their *instincts* and their feline *nature*. Curiosity.

What comes to mind when you think about things that naturally get a cat's attention? Irresistible things for cats?

- String?
- Laser light?
- Fishbowl?
- Mouse?

You are experiencing the modeling of several techniques right now.

Stay tuned . . . Be Sherlocky . . . Here they come . . .

"Tell me and I forget. Teach me and I remember. Involve me and I learn."
—Benjamin Franklin (1780)

SHOW, DON'T TELL (used in Herding Cats)

INSTEAD OF A LONG LECTURE about brain functions and anatomy that would quickly turn you off, we used a cat simile with *single words* to demonstrate **Show, Don't Tell.**

String? Laser light? Fishbowl? And bingo! Instantly your brain snatched the bait. Like Ben said, you were *involved.*

"What? What are you talking about, teacher?"

(Let's put the clues together, my friend.)

By using single words as questions, we created big *gaps* that *your* brain couldn't resist (just like *"Snap Crackle . . . ?"*).

The technique?

Fewer words leave gaps.

Your brain immediately *wants* to fill those gaps.

It's Un-Ignorable!

Your imagination was *instinctively triggered.*

(Remember Pixar? Your brain *worked* without knowing it.)

When you read *fishbowl*, it instantly triggered a tiny movie in your mind of a curious cat and a *fishbowl.* The same happened when you read *laser light* and *string*. You immediately filled in the gaps and created your own little internal movie in an instant. I just flipped the switch and . . . *Voila!*

Your brain has now become my ally.

My partner. Involved. Engaged. See?

Each time you read a single word it triggered a movie in your mind connected to a cat's nature. We used *your* instincts and *your* nature while talking about a cat.

And guess what? You now understand this concept 10 times better because we *showed it to you*, instead of trying to explain all this invisible magic. You were *Showed, Not Told*.

You will also *remember* this moment because you **experienced** the power of *Teaching in rhythm with human nature!*

> ### Fewer words leave gaps that are Un-Ignorable to the brain.

The more we use *fluffy* words, and the more we **Tell** (spoon-feed), the less they listen.

The more we **Show**, with fewer and stronger words, the more deeply they are engaged and listen intently.

Think back. How engaged were you as I personally *showed* you our concept with my magical mind-reading skills? *(wink)*

Remember our promise of *Brain Magic Revealed*? *(Itch)* You are learning the magical secrets right now. *(Scratch)*

FREEDOM   (used in Herding Cats)

ALWAYS GIVE AS MUCH FREEDOM as you can for students to create their own, personal meaning of the lesson. Creating meaning is synthesis, which is high-level critical thinking. It's extremely motivating and important to the brain, and that is exactly what we want.

Personally synthesizing information, by triggering their mental movies, dramatically improves understanding, retention, and fun in the process.

When we use *kitty*, it triggers Sara's imagination, the movie in her mind, in the same way and encourages her to create her own meaning from the information. That is the instinct of the brain. Her brain also now *becomes our ally.* (partner)

But if I try to force-feed *my* movie, their brain becomes my enemy, because I'm trying to violate its instinct to make *personal meaning*. It shuts down. Not interested. *"That's not how I see it, teacher!"*

All of this happens instantly and automatically, just by using fewer words.

*The brain needs Freedom to
create Personal Meaning.*

CLIFFHANGER   (used in Herding Cats)

*"How can we make their brain our ally,
not our enemy?"*

That simple question was used to set your mind up for a bit of intrigue, and also create a little curiosity.

(Cliffhanger/Itch)

Your brain is instinctively curious and tries to quickly solve mysteries. (Survival mechanism, principle #2)

Using curiosity and mystery makes your brain my ally.

By understanding human nature, and knowing what's *Instinctively Important* to the brain, we can align our teaching to become naturally engaging, motivating, and fun. ("I–I Captain!")

Here's what we are learning:

- **Speak less, leave gaps**
  The brain can't resist filling them. Irresistible.

- Free students to create personal meaning
  It's 100 times more Important than your version.

- **Ask mysterious questions** (Cliffhangers)
  Again, the brain can't resist trying to solve them.

  It's Magnetic.

Brain Break / Refresh

Trivia Question - If you are normally a speed reader, why are you reading this book slower?
Answer - Because it is intentionally designed to partner with the rhythm of your brain. Fewer words create Gaps to fill. Important stuff Creates Partners. Allies, not Enemies. And it's Fun for the brain instead of exhausting.
(That was another tiny brain break/refresh. Feel it?)

Everything we do together is modeling so you can feel it personally, as the student. Remember This:

Invisible things are extremely powerful.

It's not nothing.

If you like and need these Brain Break Refreshers, guess what? So will your kids! Do it for them too, teacher! The whole climate of your classroom will improve.

Be the thermostat. Not just a thermometer.

What can we do to make their brain our ally, not our enemy?

- Engage their emotions. Don't erase them.
- Change their mood, and they will change their mind (about learning).
- Use mysterious, leading questions.
- Give clues, not answers. Secretly make them work for their meal.
- Speak less, leave gaps.
  It's irresistible, magnetic, and gives . . .

- Freedom and space to create personal meaning.
- Show, Don't Tell.
- Create Cliffhangers.
- Say Important stuff, no fluff. No BS.

Teaching in rhythm with human nature immediately feels safe, true, interesting, engaging, and fun for the brain. It's Irresistible. Magnetic. Un-Ignorable. That's Albrainian.

All of these tools work together to create positive emotions that gradually become associated with you, your classroom, and most importantly, with learning.

That is a legacy I would be proud to leave.

WHO'S DRIVING?

LET'S PLAY AGAIN, my friend, just for a minute. I'll give you some prompts, and I want you to read each of them slowly, one at a time, and spend several seconds picturing each one in your mind's eye. Do your *personal best* to visualize.

But first, take a deep breath . . . slowly. Calm your mind.

Okay, ready?

First, think about this:

What do you need *to do* in your classroom?

Picture it in your mind now. Focus on it for several seconds. What do you need to do in your classroom?

Next . . .

What are your deadlines? Visualize them.

Next . . . Think about your lists for several seconds.

Next . . .

What are our responsibilities?

What are your commitments?

What do you need to do? Think about it.

Okay, pause. Take a slow, deep breath.

Now, I want you to think about your thoughts. What emotions did you feel? Think about it for a minute. How did that feel?

When I present to large groups, the answers are always the same. Overwhelmed. Stressed. Anxious.

Now, let's learn how to change that, my friend.

WHAT DO YOU *WANT?*

This time, I want you to visualize again, in the same way, and pause to slowly focus on each of the questions, one at a time.

But first, take another slow, deep breath. Ready?

Here we go:

What do you *want* your classroom to be?

If it could be anything, what would you want it to be? Focus on that. Play that movie in your mind. Visualize it.

Nex t. . .

What do you *want* your classroom to look like?

What do you *want* the climate in your room to feel like? Can you see it?

What do you *want* to offer to your kids?

What do you *want* them to look like?

Okay, pause. Take a deep breath. Now think about your thoughts. Tell me, what emotions did you feel? Think about it for a minute. How did that feel? What did you think? What did you picture?

Again, the answers I hear over and over are the same.

Happy! Motivated to achieve that vision! Excited! Hopeful!

Something else may have also happened in your brain this time. Think about it. Did new ideas start forming in your mind? You weren't even trying to find answers. You were just focusing on your goals, and your brain may have automatically started creating ways to make it happen. It was instantly ready to make it a reality.

But how?

QUESTIONS ARE THE ANSWER

THINK OF THE BRAIN as being kind of like Google Search. The questions we ask ourselves drive the results.

The brain runs on questions, like Google.

The questions we focus on steer the car.

You just experienced how the leading questions, in our visualizations, affected your mood and mind. 'Change their mood, and they will change their mind.' Remember?

You felt 2 different results based on the default "worrying" questions versus the powerful "goal-oriented" questions.

All brains naturally default to negative thoughts for safety and survival. It says, "Better safe than sorry!"

The way to override that negative default is to instantly replace it with positive goals and to remember our past successes.

Another example:

Have you ever said something that you regretted immediately? You were tired, frustrated, hangry. It just slipped out, and then it was too late. It can't be taken back, and you can't get it out of your mind. *"Why was I so mean and dumb?!"* We've both been there.

Here's the point: As we repeat that question in our head, it's like typing it into our brain's Google search. With that question comes a presupposition. *"I am mean and dumb."*

Google, or our brain, then searches by keywords to come up with an answer. When we ask a lousy question, we get a lousy answer: *Because you are a jerk and an idiot.*

Why am I mean and dumb? Logical answer: jerk and idiot. That's very simplistic, but it's kind of how the brain works.

But that's not the answer we were looking for. It's not what we meant. It wasn't the right question. Just like focusing on and worrying about all of our struggles, doesn't bring us the help we are looking for. Like you said earlier, it makes us feel overwhelmed, stressed, and anxious.

Then what is a better question in our example? Try this: *"How can I be more positive and profound?"*

Key words—positive and profound. That now becomes our presupposition. *"I am positive and profound. How can I be even better?"*

Ask a better question, get a better answer. *Consider others' feelings and think before you speak.* Bingo! That's the help and encouragement I was looking for.

The questions used in our visualizations were intentionally chosen to lead the brain to two different destinations. One negative, then one positive. You felt the real results.

The brain runs on questions.
Questions guide the brain better than GPS.

If I accidentally take a wrong exit and end up in a very dangerous place, why would I keep taking it in the future?

It's like a sad song stuck in your head. If you know that song makes you sad, why would you choose to play it on repeat? Why wouldn't you change the station and play a song that takes you where you *want* to go?

We can't just erase a thought; we have to replace it.

CAN'T ERASE IT—GOTTA REPLACE IT

When that sad song or negative thought gets stuck in our head, we need to stop and ask, *"Who's driving?"* and become aware of our default negative thoughts. Become aware. *"Why am I taking that same lousy exit again?"*

Then we can choose a better *song*, or better question, to guide our mind to a better place and get better answers.

"What do I want? Who do I want to be? What do I want my class to be? What do I want for my students?"

This is how to partner with the brain. This is Albrainian.

Questions drive and guide the brain. They point it in a specific direction. It then immediately begins to look for the answers and make them a reality. It even works in the background, and also when we are sleeping. So choose the earworm *song* you play carefully, my friend.

We've always heard, "Say it in the positive."

Now you know how and why.

Questions work for us and for our students. We choose. Teach them. Tell them. Model. Practice. Over and over. It takes time and repetition to erase and replace embedded thoughts. But it absolutely can be done. It's a physical, biological fact.

I hope this helps you and your students, my friend.

Our lives follow the path of our strongest thoughts. Gratitude leads to happiness.

NOTES TO SELF . . .

CLIMATE CONTROL

I've come to the frightening conclusion that I am the decisive element in the classroom. It's my personal approach that creates the climate. It's my daily mood that makes the weather. As a teacher, I possess a tremendous power to make a child's life miserable or joyous.
—Haim Ginott

#7 SECRET PRINCIPLE of the Brain:

Climate Control

Be the Thermostat, not a Thermometer.

THIS IS #7 BECAUSE it is the most nuanced and subtle. It also combines everything that we have learned and more. It is invisible, yet palpable. Like closing your eyes and feeling the sun on your skin. You can just *feel* it.

Have you ever met someone, and before they said a word, you sensed that they were a really good person? Have you ever walked into a school for the first time and knew right away that it was not a happy place?

Remember early on, when we learned the brain ranks and rates everything instantly by importance? Remember our glimpse of the brain talking to itself? *(Wink)* p.42

Well, *everything instantly* includes every non-verbal clue, as well as all environmental clues; all of our intuition.

Brain Break / Refresh

> ***Pro Tip:***
> *Smell, or scent, (our olfactory sense) is one of the most memorable and powerful triggers in the brain. The way people and places Smell makes an extremely powerful impression. Good or bad*

MORE TAMBOURINE, LESS LEAD SINGER

WHO USUALLY PLAYS TAMBOURINE in a band? The backup singer. It's a *backup* or *supporting* role. But . . . what does the lead singer do during the guitar solo? He grabs a tambourine. He supports the soloist.

Teachers are almost always the lead singer in the classroom. We hate to give up the mic. We can't stop talking. *(Hint— that's not the most effective teaching method.)*

So, for the *band* to thrive, we also need to play the supporting role and let others solo.

Great teachers lift people. Others' success is our success. Our goal should be to create lead singers, and that doesn't happen without a lot of repetition. Regrettably, a lot of teachers have never learned to give up the mic and play tambourine.

What percentage of class time do teachers talk compared to students?

On average, what do you think?

What do you think is the optimal percentage for most effective learning?

Guess?

Now, stop for a minute and look up "Teacher talk time" and discover for yourself. Then come right back.

Also, consider this: good relationships often have two roles—*flower* and *gardener*—and good partners take turns. Most people would not choose to always and only be the gardener and never the flower.

Deep Thought

Do we ask our students to be the *gardeners* of our Agendas, and never be the *flower*?　　　　*(Ouch!)*

Yes, teachers must play a huge leadership role in the classroom. But we also claim the part of the gardener, while mostly being the flower.

A real gardener cares for the flower by giving it what it needs, not giving what the gardener needs. If she loves to water, does she drown the plants? If she loves cultivating, does she chop the roots? If she loves the sun (spotlight), does she block their shine?

"But Steven, I have to do most of the talking because I have so much to cover and it takes too long to let students collaborate, plus . . . the behavior problems!"

You've heard this:

> *If you always do what you've always done,*
> *you'll always get what you always got.*
> My twist . . .
> *If you always think what you've always thought,*
> *you'll always get what you always got.*

Did you look up teacher talk time?

I attempted to make it important enough for you (by using a bit of curiosity).

If you didn't, it means that I didn't, and that you felt and experienced the same lack of motivation that your students feel every day.

And that point leads us straight to the type of self-deception that we have been talking about from the beginning. We say to ourselves:

> *"But I did make it important—kids just*
> *don't care about anything today."*

Not really. I'm fooling myself. My bit of curiosity was a nice start for a little engagement, but too weak to move you to action. *More my fault than yours.* I ignored your brain's instincts. Remember Principles 1 and 2?

1) Importance Drives Everything
2) Survival First

My little bit of curiosity wasn't a VIP (wasn't very important), and the boss (brain) refuses to waste vital energy on trivia (for Survival).

Always Remember:

*The brain runs on a few basic principles
that can't be broken.*

We can either use them for good, or fight them and fail.

Solution:

Make it **Instinctively Important** enough for them. ("I–I Captain!")

How?

One option is to **Tell them why.**

Continually.

Like this:

You already know that if you make the effort to look up the answer about *teacher talk time* for yourself, it will be more memorable and more meaningful for you.

But I didn't tell you that it may be as much
as *10 times* more. 10 times more.

You will be 10 times more likely to remember it, use it in your classroom, engage your kids, and reduce behavior problems and apathy. It really is that Important. No joke.

(Psst . . . Motivation and Retention are
giant keys to successful learning.)

These things are how we teach in rhythm with the instincts of the brain. This is how we play tambourine. This is how we take our turn being the gardener and giving the flower what it needs; by making it **Instinctively Important**. ("I–I Captain!")

Here comes the Reveal. . .

Studies show that teachers, on average, talk about 80% of the time during class, and students around 20%. Optimal learning is, sadly, approximately the inverse. 80% student discussion (on task), and 20% teacher talk.

Think about sitting through one of your billions of professional development training sessions, listening to a presenter who took lessons from Charlie Brown's teacher. How valuable was that for you?

How much more valuable would it have been if you were given the important information from the training and then allowed to collaborate, discuss, and brainstorm with your grade-level team?

Our message is clear. Being a true gardener in the classroom means giving the flower what it needs, not just what *we* like or need to get done.

And not just token efforts to soothe our conscience, like my bit of curiosity that didn't move you.

If it wouldn't move you, it won't move them either.

All of this means giving up the mic, learning to play tambourine, and giving our students more reps as the lead singer. That's how we teach in rhythm with the brain.

BURIED TREASURE
(from the above...)
We all tend to teach the way we like to *learn*. But...

**If we only teach the way *we* like to learn,
We only reach students who are just like us.**

"Education is not the filling of a vessel,
but the lighting of a fire."
—Plutarch (Teacher/Philosopher—115 AD)

One of the greatest injustices we can commit
is to pass on our limitations to our children.

I hate using Arts & Crafts in teaching.

And that's why I keep using them.

BE PERPETUALLY PLEASANT AND UNPERTURBABLE

Be stable. Unshakable. Solid as a rock. Immovable. The wind and rain can beat against the mountain and it does not crumble. Don't lose your temper or become shocked and incredulous. Be Curious, Not Furious.

Be the grown-up in the building. You can handle the challenges and problems. When students break the rules, simply refer back to them and the preset consequences. Call 'em like a referee. Unphased. On to the next play.

Your consistency and maturity and stability will be contagious. They will begin to imitate your model when they deal with their own challenges. *"We can handle it, learn from it, and move forward without bitterness."*

"I never lose. I either win, or learn."
—Nelson Mandela

When the leader shows this kind of calm, assertive strength under pressure, it becomes the norm for all.

Do all you can to make *"Doing Right"* **easy** and *"Doing Wrong"* **difficult**. Place guardrails and incentives on the right path and roadblocks on the wrong path.

Lubricate *doing right.*

Don't Irritate or Provoke to Anger
when *wrong* does happen.

Call 'em like a referee . . .

Penalty = 'x' minutes in the penalty box.

Foul = 2 shots.

Out of bounds = turnover

Holding = 10 yards and loss of down.

Etc . . .

Then walk away, and on to the next play. It's over.
Move on.

Don't Irritate or Provoke to Anger
when *wrong* does happen.

PART THREE
WORKING YOUR MAGIC

FROM APATHY TO AMBITION
The Top 3 Brain Secrets to Motivate Lazy Learners

Kids haven't been taught to Stick With It! Keep Going. Push Through. Grow Stronger. Develop Determination. Heart.

If teaching is merely about content delivery and explaining, then we have already been replaced by the internet, social media, YouTube, and others.

But if teachers connect real-life experiences with personal coaching, to continually improve their students' *Personal Best*—then they will never be replaced.

Here's exactly how you can do that . . .

From Apathy to Ambition is a guide developed for my graduate classes, to help kids grow in these areas. It's too big for this book, but I want you to have it, as my gift to you, when you sign up for our fresh and free 1-Minute Engagement Tips, Activities, and Articles at EngagingEducatorsToday. com. Click Here to Join Us!

It includes tons of practical ideas to help you teach and model a Growth Mindset. It was a most requested piece in my classes, and it will have lots of value for you.

And if you find this book valuable, please help us spread the word with a quick review on Amazon.

It's *Super Important* for us! Thank you! (*smiles*)

AN APP IS OPEN

I like being a beginner. I like doing something for the first time; Not knowing what to do, and saying, "Let's figure it out."

It is challenging, but also exciting.

Teachers are life-long learners and often feel the same way. But, why? Why would anyone feel excited about learning something that is undoubtedly going to be a struggle? Others would say, "That's not my idea of fun."

So, why do we enjoy learning when it can be challenging and awkward?

What do you think? Hmmm . . . That's a Deep Thought. *(smiles)*

I'll let you ponder that and we'll come back to it in a minute.

***** (change of subject)

Did you know that the brain loves to learn things in little bite-sized pieces?

Memory and brain experts call this concept *chunking,* and since the brain loves it so much, we'll be using it to tackle some of our own complicated topics one little bite at a time; small, simple steps that you really can use tomorrow.

Though we both know how hard it is to make complex things simple, it is well worth the work for our students.

Great teachers everywhere do that very thing, each and every day. We use *chunking* every day to break our content into small, easy-to-understand pieces.

Until we are rushed and short on time. Which is . . . almost always. Then sometimes we slip into the dreaded *Data Dumping*. Just food for thought, my friend.

See "How to Stop Data Dumping" on our free blog at EngagingEducatorsToday.com

(. . . in order to keep this *chunk* small . . . modeling)

***** (change of subject)

By the way, did you also know that your brain works in the background to answer questions? All the time? It's kind of like a Google search app running in the background that never sleeps. (Hint: That's one more way that we can speak Albrainian every day.)

NOTE TO SELF! ***** Remember to use, and take advantage of, the brain's natural "back-channel" learning app. But how? In the same way we are modeling right now.

Introduce a concept, then ask a question. Get them thinking about it, then briefly change the subject to something lighter. Come back to the question a little later.

Learning experts call this *Spaced Learning*, and it has been shown to be highly effective for increasing retention. We are also using another technique called *Interleaving*. Look it up. It's good stuff.

We've both personally felt this "back-channel" problem-solving app thingy in real time, and know it to be true.

Has this ever happened to you? A song comes on and you can't remember who sings it. Five minutes later, you are talking about something else, and the name pops into your head. How does that happen?

Answer: Your brain continued to look for the answer in the background, even when you were talking about other things.

Bonus Trivia—

Our brain does a ton of this kind of "back-channel" thinking while we are sleeping. It accomplishes things like problem-solving, organizing thoughts and memories, and creative thinking. All while we are snoozing away. It's crazy and amazing stuff! And also, why sleep is so important!

When we use these ideas in our teaching, our kids will enjoy it, their brains will love it, stress will begin to melt, and retention and comprehension will increase.

***** (change of subject)

Now, let's go back to our original question: *"Why do we enjoy learning when it can be challenging and awkward?"*

Of course, there are many reasons, but here's one that you may not have come up with:

Teachers are weird.

We think too much. We love to think about, and analyze invisible things. We actually tend to overthink everything. Teachers are *Master Overthinkers*.

It's an occupational hazard, because our job requires us to blend our thinking with our students' thinking to create new thinking, so we constantly try to read their minds and find better ways to communicate.

(Only teachers can follow that . . . *wink*)

It's an impossible task, but when we get it right, it's a magical, musical thing.

We love it when our kids light up. And that's a great reason we love learning, even though it's hard.

We have also realized that learning *requires* making mistakes that make us better. And we know that empowers us to help more people. That's definitely worth the challenge, and probably one of the reasons you are reading this book.

Bonus Point

Another reason that people enjoy learning is that *the brain naturally seeks challenges* in order to grow stronger. We have a hard-wired survival instinct to solve problems, get smarter, and grow stronger to stay alive.

The brain instinctively knows this fact:

The more we do, the more we can do.

The less we do, the less we can do.

In a Nutshell

Here's what we're learning:

- *Point #1*—The brain loves to learn in simple, little, bite-sized pieces of information and *time*. Remember: This applies to shorter amounts of *time* as well as *information* (more on that later). Do you remember what this concept is called?

- *Point #2*—The brain never stops thinking and working and problem-solving *in the background*, even when we are distracted, and especially when we are sleeping.

- *Point #3*—The brain can learn to enjoy a struggle that leads to a greater goal (that's called a Growth Mindset).

- **Bonus Point:** When you teach these 3 concepts to your students, and use them yourself, engagement will happen automatically, along with other improvements across the board.

*Extra Bonus Point

The brain loves, and needs, a nice Goldilocks Challenge.

Not too hard   (that feels hopeless)

Not too easy   (that's boring)

Juuust Right   (keeps us engaged & feels rewarding)

Reminder: You can begin using and teaching these things to your kids tomorrow, and it will begin to change the way they think and learn. Kids love to learn this stuff. It will also change how they look at, and listen to, you.

*FREE Extra, Extra Bonus Point:

Kids love to learn how *their brain* works. So, Tell Them.

Don't just implement all these great ideas and then forget to explain them to your students. ***Remember to Tell Them what you are doing, and why.***

We all want and need to know why we are being asked to do something. Knowing helps us to buy in and remember. It only takes a second. Give it a try and see what happens. They will appreciate it. Just like you.

"There is no learning without remembering."
—Socrates

It's nearly impossible for the brain to remember something we can't connect with. If we can't apply and use what we learn, the brain will instinctively delete it as a survival mechanism.

So, *Tell Them* what they are learning, and *Why*. (It's so easy to forget the *Why*.) **Not knowing how to convince students to buy-in is the Achilles' heel for most teachers. And that's one of the knowledge gaps we are here to fill today.**

NOTICE   NOTICE

- I am doing that for you now, and have been, throughout our time together here.
- So, each time we pause to explain Why we are doing something . . .
- Notice it. Be aware of it. Think about it. And. . .
- Analyze how it raises *your* motivation 1%.

BE PROFOUND

Like this:

> *Speak Less,*
> *Yet Say More.*

> *If you want things to change*
> *around you -*
> **Be Different**.

Be Quotable.

(. . . I said, *"Be Quotable"*. . .

as a quote . . .

it's kind of like a double . . .

never mind)

USE 'AND'—NOT 'BUT'

'And' adds. *'But'* erases.

This is so simple. Easy. Invisible. And has Life-Changing Power! It can change the weather in your classroom.

Once in a while, *'but'* is the appropriate choice. *But* most of the time, (see what I did there?) *'and'* is exponentially better.

"I love your energy Jose, but we really need to focus now."

Versus

"I love your energy Jose, and when you focus it, you are one of our hardest workers!"

'But' erases. It makes the encouragement false and takes it away completely. Pulls you in, then pushes you down. Brutal.

'And' adds. It reinforces and builds. Pulls you in, then builds you up and makes you stronger.

In order to experience this personally and feel how powerful it can be, stop and take a minute to visualize the love of your life saying "and" versus "but."

"I love you, and . . ."

Or

"I love you, but . . ."

Use 'And'—Not 'But'.

NOTES TO SELF

Einstein believed that experiencing *mystery* was the
most beautiful thing . . . and that *wonder* was the

fundamental emotion that creates
all true art and true science.

TEACH LIKE A LEARNER

***Great teachers never lose their wonder,
or their thirst for truth and wisdom.***

They continually display their *curiosity and awe*. They are
driven to discover, and learn new things. And they remind
themselves that *real learning* is a unique conjuring of magic,
in each individual mind.

When we forget to use these mysteries and magic, we
become no more memorable than Google Search; just pouring millions of answers on top of the brain and hoping
something soaks in. But we know that's the opposite of
how learning happens in the mind.

Remember that every new moment of learning is scary . . .
and exciting. A vulnerable, first-time adventure for the brain.
In a way, every new lesson requires each student to be a
Beginner! That's a tough spot to constantly be forced into!

Whenever we learn something new, a tiny little *thought* is
born, and can be seen in real-time on a brain scan today.
Each delicate new *idea* struggles to survive and carve
its own path through a tangled jungle of a million other
thoughts and opinions. It's a difficult thing. It takes a lot

of energy, and this fragile new piece of *learning* can easily get lost, lose heart, and give up.

When the brain is overwhelmed with too much too fast, it simply shuts down. Zero learning happens. We just want to give up, go home, and be safe.

The brain needs, no, *has to* have *time*, to create new meaning and to make new associations (connections) with prior knowledge.

It takes time. We can't change that—and we need to stop trying. Forcing more and more, only makes things worse.

It's like this: If we don't give enough time, the mind will take its toys and go home. It will check out.

We've both been there 1000s of times ourselves, sitting in a class or workshop, hating it. The teacher is water torture. It's Hopeless. Never-ending. We *know* how painful it is, and how nothing sticks when more and more keeps pouring in.

So why do *we* keep falling into that trap?

Remember this:

> ## CLICK *SAVE*
>
> When you want them to keep, and remember, the work and the lesson, you must **CLICK *SAVE*** and wait for their cursor to stop spinning. If you yank the plug without saving, all your work is lost.

Give *Think Time*
(and a 2-minute *Debrief* at the end of every lesson)

One way is to **Use a Simple Prompt** to help them write down their thoughts for 2 minutes.

Then they could trade with a partner for 1 minute.

You know 1000 different ways. It's not hard, nor long. The point is that *It Must be done.* Don't forget. Just Do It.

CLICK SAVE before you pull the plug and switch lessons. Don't forget, or you'll lose all your hard work! It's Albrainian.

"But Steven, I do give think-time. Well . . .

Sometimes I just need to get one more thing in before the bell. The test is coming up. Plus, they get out of control if I don't keep pouring."

It's crazy to keep doing the same thing and expect a different result. So:

*If you want things around you to change, **Be Different.***

But we just keep pouring more and faster, trying to solve the wrong problem. We keep asking ourselves, "How can I get more done, faster?"

Wrong question.

Pouring more, and faster, is not the answer. And we both know it in our hearts. **Retention** is the key to *progress.* And Retention only comes with focused Attention.

Right now is the perfect time to reset our mindset and methods. The pandemic shuffled the deck and everyone is working with a new hand. The old is gone, so let's play this new hand in a new and better way.

Benchmarks and culture are all being reset, so why not set them right? Teach the *important* things that have the most value for your kids.

Let's slip off the handcuffs of our executive ivory-tower non-teachers. Instead, let's embrace what truly works in rhythm with the brain, and with real learning.

Teach Lincoln like this:

> *"Let me tell you about a guy whose mother died when he was nine.*
>
> *His first girlfriend got sick and she died.*
>
> *Later, he became president."*

End the lesson like this:

> *"Here's something few people in the world know:*
>
> *Lincoln was the first president ever to be photographed at his inauguration. And John Wilkes Booth (his assassin) can be seen standing behind Lincoln in the picture.*

(Super Creepy!)

> *True story—check it out."*

That image will stick forever.

That's how to *Work Your Magic* in Rhythm with the Brain.

JOB SUCCESS

Research conducted by Harvard university,
the Carnegie Foundation, and Stanford
Research Center, has all concluded that over 50%
of *job success* comes from having
well-developed communication skills and people skills.

The Field Trip

Setting: An all-day 8th grade field trip—I was in charge.

2,000 Jr/Sr high kids from all over, flooded the university campus that day.

Our chaperones were each in charge of 5 students. Tons of activities were available, and groups were going in different directions. Several whole group meet-ups were scheduled throughout the day.

It was a beautiful day, and everyone was having a great time.

Until *3:47 p.m.*

I always had my group at the meet-ups early—just in case.

While scanning the crowd for our groups to arrive, I saw some of them running toward me . . . with campus security.

A teacher's worst nightmare.

"Shannon is missing! One second she was right there with us, then the next . . ."

A thousand questions brought no answers. Security, police, and all of us began the search.

53 minutes later:

Shannon arrived at our meet-up site, laughing, with her brand-new boyfriend from another school. Part of a pattern for her. Fast forward a few years . . .

19 years later:

I was working the door at a home basketball game when a young woman came up to me.

"Mr. N! I was hoping to catch you. I was in town and heard there was a game tonight. I wanted to let you know that I am married, and we have a new baby boy.

"And I just really wanted you to know that I turned out alright."

Shannon hugged me and cried, saying,

"And I wanted to thank you for making me feel safe, even when things got really crazy. I'm so sorry."

We can never know how or when things might change.

Tough Kids

I was eating at McDonald's one day when a professional-looking young man walked up and said,

"Hey Mr. N! How are you?"

At that point in my career, I had long ago given up trying to recognize every former student decades later.

"I'm good buddy, but you're going to have to help me with your name."

"I'm Neal—remember me?"

Shock, Red-Alert, and Confusion flooded my brain. Neal was the most dangerous student I've ever had. I never turned my back. I fully expected him to be in prison before graduating.

"Can I sit down for a minute? I'd love to catch up."

"Sure . . . Neal . . . have a seat."

Neal has a Ph.D. in psychology and works with troubled teens.

His turnaround had nothing to do with me.

Here's my point:

We can never predict how a student will turn out.

Or what might trigger an entire life change.

For better or worse.

So stop predicting.

Just plant the best seeds you have—every day.

JUDGE YOUR JUDGMENT

Our judgment might be right—based on what we know, but . . .

There's always a lot we don't know.

There are always 2 sides.

Ancient proverb:

"It is a foolish king who passes judgment

after hearing only one side of the story."

The view from the other side can look very different.

The Famous Side

The 'Back' Side

Consider this statement: *"I don't care to do that."*

What does that mean? Think about it. When I ask large groups, most agree that it is a polite refusal.

But in the South, it means the opposite. It means,

"Sure, I don't mind doing that."

Remember:

There's always a lot we don't know. Or understand. Always 2 sides.   *Judge your Judgment.*

The view from the other side can look very different.

> **Good judgment is learned from experience—**
> **a lot of which comes from bad judgment.**

So, the next time a firestorm starts, and it is blasting you in the face—Stop. Take a deep breath. Then remind yourself to be *Sherlocky* instead.

These are my thoughts in times like these:

Be Curious, Not Furious.
Fighting Fire with Fire Only Builds a Bigger Fire.

When the flames are flaming and burning your face, don't stare at them. Look for the *source* of the fire. Aim the extinguisher at the base. That's how to douse a fire.

When an angry parent walks in attacking, and you don't have a clue what's going on, rise above it, and be curious.

"Okay, let's slow down. I don't know what you're talking about. Is your daughter okay?"

(looking for the source)

"No, she's Not okay! How can you even?!?!"

(More rant, more flames!)

Sometimes, simply letting the storm rage, without speaking, can weaken and calm things. Stay strong, curious, and undeterred.

It's not about you.

It's about finding the thorn in the lion's paw.

Emotions are very contagious. Don't catch the parent's anger. Let him catch your solution-seeking, calm, positive energy.

Tossing water at the flames just turns to steam, accomplishes very little, and runs you out of water. Save it to douse the source when you find it.

Be Curious, Not Furious.

Listen carefully for clues to discern the true source of the pain.

> "First and foremost, you need to know that your child is very important to me too, and that I absolutely want the very best for her. We both want that. We are on the same page.

Now let's talk. What exactly did she tell you?

Help me understand. . ."

Stephen Covey says,

"Seek first to understand, then to be understood."

And also,

"Listen with the intent to understand,
not with the intent to respond."

Find, and aim the extinguisher at, the source.

And remember to *Judge your Judgment.* View, and study it, from both sides.   That's wisdom.

(Hint, hint: These things work great with students, too.

And all human beings. It's Albrainian.) (*Wink*)

"We're all broken. That's how the light gets in."
—Ernest Hemingway.

When someone comes to us in genuine pain, it's an opportunity to bring in a bit of light and grow a relationship.

Even if we still disagree in the end, respect can grow with better understanding, proven compassion, truth, and empathy.

You may also need to say,

"I won't be talked to that way.
When you are ready to talk calmly, let me know."

Then walk away. You've done the best you can.

Stay strong, and Always take the high road, my friend. It's hard. But, take it from this teacher who is a few years ahead, you will never look back and regret having character and integrity.

CREATING THE MAGNETIC CLASSROOM

MAGNETS ARE ATTRACTED to *steel*.

Not aluminum. Not pot-metal (fake steel) or plastic.

Magnets are attracted to, pull toward, *Real Steel.*

Every student is a magnet.

They **instinctively pull** what they **want** into their brain.

That's Albrainian. (All brains do—universal)

(Principles #1—**I**mportant to us. And #2—Survival.)

We all do it.

Our level of Engagement with any new information (content) or person shows the strength of our *Magnetic Pull toward it.*

One of our goals is to strengthen their pull toward us, and toward the content.

But how?

By personally being the most premium, purest, and strongest *steel*. By being driven to discover and seek truth. Truth is compelling and *Instictively Important. (I–I, Captain!)*

Magnets don't stick to aluminum.

Or fake steel.

The magnet immediately knows the quality of the metal, and if it isn't *Real Steel* it simply falls off. It's automatic and immediate.

It simply falls off of fake steel.

And the brain instinctively and immediately turns off and falls off of fake people.

Everything we say must be 'Real Steel.'

The fake rationalizations and *advice* from our "executives" in ivory towers don't stick.

They simply do not cut it in real life.

We have talked a lot about how people make decisions based on emotions.

Our feelings. Our gut. Our intuitions. Remember?

Well, those are exactly the pieces of the puzzle that engage, or disengage, our students.

They decide to participate (or disrupt) based on their emotions.

Based on their gut. Based on how much they are *pulled* toward us and the content.

And how strong their *magnetic pull* is toward the purity, quality, and strength of our 'metal.'

They can smell it a mile away. In seconds.

Authenticity. Value. **Scarcity**.

High Quality People are rare. **Scarce**.

Scarcity = Valuable.

Valuable = Engaging.

Engaging creates a 'Magnetic Pull.'

They want to *pull* what we have into their brains.

It's Albrainian for Survival. Un-Ignorable.

When they *know* that everything we do and say wishes them well, and is for their best benefit and success, then, they will walk through fire for us.

> *"People don't care how much you know, until they know how much you care."*
> *—Teddy Roosevelt.*

President Theodore Roosevelt said that.

The Rough-Rider.

Not Dr. Phil.

The man who charged up the hill and took it, in a bloody battle that led men to their deaths.

And they followed him.

Because of that very conviction.

"But how do we do that in our classroom?"

Be honest, and tell them straight. Especially the tough kids. Like this:

> *"Alan, I want you to win more than you can imagine. I want to help you win. I want you to grow real strength and courage. To succeed and laugh and be happy. And I will also do everything I can to protect you from pain— even if it makes you mad! I'm going to show you the landmines, and tell you the danger, and even push you away if you are about to step on one. I'm going to do everything I can to protect you and help you win. But it won't happen if you keep fighting against it. If you fight to keep pain and failure in your life, that's what will eventually happen. Only you can make that choice and decision."*

STUDENT PULL vs TEACHER PUSH

It's time now for an educational paradigm shift. We need to change teaching from a *push* model to a *pull* model.

Pushing data doesn't work in rhythm with the instincts of the brain. It violates them.

> *When we violate, or ignore the instincts*
> *of the brain, learning suffers.*

Creating a magnetic *pull from the students* creates desire, motivation, and ownership of learning within each student.

That's when valuable new meaning is created in the brain.

It was 2 days before a long vacation trip,
and my grass was already way too high,
when my lawn mower died. 'Great!'
So, I YouTubed it. I got the answer,
Amazoned the part, and fixed it the next day.
One vacation stressor erased.

And that new knowledge stuck. I won't forget.

That's a *pull* learning model. Today's Learning Model.

I *needed* it. It was *Important*. I *pulled* the info. Learned it. Used it. And will remember it. Forever.

Pushing irrelevant data no longer works.

Irrelevant information is . . . Irrelevant.

(Tangential info is still vital!)
But that's a topic for another time . . .

Our job is to lead and create the *right* magnetic *pull*.

(Desire. Interest. Need.)

Like this:

"Hey kids, did you know that the more well-spoken you are,
the more money you'll make? It's the Green *Language! Fact."*

They can do the rest (mostly) if they want to. Or *have* to. Like me with the mower.

I know this may sound like crazy talk to you, but it is the world we find ourselves in today.

Look, if a seasoned guy like me can figure this out, you definitely can.

I've been a public school teacher and educational outlier (rebel) my entire 40+ year career. And a coach. And a musician/band leader. And a teacher-trainer.

(see references in the introduction)

And . . .

I am still convinced, after studying the greatest teachers today and throughout history, along with the newest brain science, plus practicing for decades—that *Lighting the Fire* is the most important element in education.

Creating the student *pull* instead of

forcing the teacher *push.*

*"But, how do I become **Real Steel?**"*

Teach in Rhythm with their Brain.

Stop focusing on the "What,"

and focus on their "Why."

(It's the kindling for their fire)

Real teaching is not about filling a brain—
it's about lighting a fire.

And make no mistake—I'm not idealistic. I know all too well what it's like with parents, admins, and students that truly don't care.

I'm not saying this will fix all your problems.

We both know we can't force good choices or change others. We can only offer a good influence.

> *"You cannot push someone up a ladder*
> *if they are unwilling to climb."*
> —*Andrew Carnegie*

The best thing we can do is to set a great standard, stick to it, teach the consequences of actions and choices, allow them to choose their own fate, and then call 'em like a referee. Without malice.

A LITTLE SONG

Our goal today is to help you be more effective, engaging, interesting, and valuable to your students.

Teaching in rhythm with your students' brains and human nature will alleviate many classroom management problems. We both know that teaching well is all about relationships. And it will also engage the music in their mind.

Music speaks to our heart and mind in a way nothing else does because the ways of the mind Are musical, rhythmic, and harmonious.

Einstein was also a musician, and said the music of his mind led him to the Theory of Relativity.

He felt the rhythm of his thoughts, or the *Little Song*, in his head. And it revealed great mysteries to him.

A teacher is a conductor who tunes each student in to the *Little Song* of Learning, inside their mind and heart.

Sadly, yes, some will continue to choose chaos and anarchy as their motif. No doubt.

But *we* will choose, and teach, harmony, wisdom, and joy. Every day.

GRAND FINALE

One of the greatest gifts I've ever received came from a teenager at the end of my 2nd year of teaching. He said:

"You are the teacher I'm going to tell my grandkids about."

I can hear it, and see it, like it was yesterday. Just 3 seconds in time, over 40 years ago . . . that became a guide for my entire career.

In that moment, I saw how powerful words can be. How what we do, and say, matters, and can last for generations. I saw my words living on in his life, and his in mine.

I also realized that the power had come from somehow connecting with his human nature. But how? I've been searching for the answer ever since.

40 years later (and wiser), I am writing to you with the hope of empowering you to create that same type of natural connection that gives life to your words.

Be more than an excellent explainer.

Be a true educator.

Engage the music of their minds

and change their lives.

I wish you the very best success, my friend.

Steven

RESOURCES

Ambrose, Susan, Michael Bridges, and Marsha Lovett. *How Learning Works: 7 Research-Based Principles for Smart Teaching*. San Francisco: John Wiley and Sons, 2010.

Amen, Daniel G., and Tana Amen. *The Brain Warrior's Way: Ignite Your Energy and Focus, Attack Illness and Aging, Transform Pain into Purpose*. New York: Berkley, 2017.

Anderson, Mike. *The Well-Balanced Teacher: How to Work Smarter and Stay Sane Inside the Classroom and Out*. Alexandria, VA: Association for Supervision and Curriculum Development (ASCD), 2010.

Ashman, Greg. *The Truth About Teaching an Evidence-Informed Guide for New Teachers*. Los Angeles, Calif: Sage, 2018.

Bender, William N. *20 Disciplinary Strategies for Working With Challenging Students*. West Palm Beach, FL: Learning Sciences International, 2016.

Bennett, Tom. *Running The Room: The Teacher's Guide to Behaviour*. Woodbridge: John Catt Educational, 2020.

Bloomberg. (2010b, May 18). *What Chief Executives Really Want*. https://www.bloomberg.com/news/ articles/2010-05-18/what-chief-executives-really-want

Bruyckere, De Pedro, and Daniel T. Willingham. *The Ingredients for Great Teaching*. London ; Los Angeles: SAGE, 2018.

Canfield, Jack, and Harold C. Wells. *100 Ways to Enhance Self-Concept in The Classroom: A Handbook for Teachers and Parents*. Boston: Allyn and Bacon, 1992.

Carey, Benedict. *How We Learn the Surprising Truth About When, Where and Why It Happens*. New York: Random House, 2015.

Carrithers, Michael. *Why Humans Have Cultures: Explaining Anthropology and Social Diversity*. New York, NY: Oxford University Press, 2010.

Chenoweth, Karin. *Schools That Succeed: How Educators Marshal the Power of Systems for Improvement*. Cambridge, MA: Harvard Education Press, 2017.

Christodoulou, Daisy. *Seven Myths About Education*. London: Routledge, 2014.

Cialdini, Robert B. *Influence the Psychology of Persuasion*. New York: Harper Business, 2021.

"Correlational Study between Eight Teacher Effectiveness Indicators and Teacher Pupil Control Ideology Characteristics." 1991, https://core.ac.uk/download/215295228.pdf.

Covey, Stephen R. *The 7 Habits of Highly Effective People: Powerful Lessons in Personal Change (anniversary)*. Simon & Schuster, 2013.

Creativity is the Number One Leadership Competency — THNK School. https://www.thnk.org/blog/creativity-is-the-way-forward-for-successful-enterprise/

Dalio, Ray. *Principles For Success*. New York: Avid Reader PR, 2019.

Einstein, Albert, and Alan Harris. *The World as I See It. by Albert Einstein, translated by Alan Harris*. New York: Philosophical Library, 1949.

Elliott, Julian. *Motivation, Engagement and Educational Performance: International Perspectives on the Contexts for Learning*. New York: Palgrave Macmillan, 2006.

Graves, Donald H., and Nancie Atwell. *Teaching Day By Day: 180 Stories to Help You Along the Way*. Portsmouth, NH: Heinemann, 2004.

Harris, Bryan. *17 Things Resilient Teachers Do: (And 4 Things They Hardly Ever Do)*. New York: Routledge, Taylor & Francis Group, 2021.

Hattie, John. *Visible Learning for Teachers: Maximizing Impact on Learning*. London: Routledge, 2019.

Hendrick, Carl, Robin Macpherson, and Oliver Caviglioli. *What Does This Look Like in The Classroom?: Bridging the Gap Between Research and Practice*. West Palm Beach (Florida, Estados Unidos): Learning Sciences International, 2019.

Hollins, Peter. *How to Teach Anything: Break Down Complex Topics and Explain With Clarity, While Keeping Engagement and Motivation*. Peter Hollins, 2021.

Howard, Kat. *Stop Talking About Wellbeing: A Pragmatic Approach to Teacher Workload*. London: John Catt, 2020.

How to Motivate Students. http://teachersindex.com/how-to-motivate-students.html

Kotler, S. (2023). *The Art of Impossible: A Peak Performance Primer*. Harper Wave, an imprint of HarperCollinsPublishers.

Lemov, Doug. *Teach Like a Champion 49 Techniques That Put Students on The Path to College*. San Francisco: Jossey-Bass, 2010.

Leslie, Ian. *Curious: The Desire to Know & Why Your Future Depends On It*. London: Quercus, 2015.

Linsin, Michael. *Dream Class: How to Transform Any Group of Students Into The Class You've Always Wanted*. San Diego, CA: JME Publishing, 2014.

Lock, Stuart, and Tom Bennett. *The Researched Guide to Leadership: An Evidence-Informed Guide for Teachers*. Melton, Woodbridge: John Catt, 2020.

Lockyer, Stephen. *100 Ideas for Primary Teachers*. London: Bloomsbury Publishing PLC, 2018.

Mandela, Nelson. *Nelson Mandela, The Struggle is My Life: His Speeches and Writings Brought Together With Historical Documents and Accounts of Mandela in Prison by Fellow-Prisoners.* New York: Pathfinder Press, 2013.

Marzano, Robert J. *Classroom Management That Works: Facilitator's Guide.* Alexandria, VA: Association for Supervision and Curriculum Development, 2004.

Maslow, Abraham H. *A Theory of Human Motivation: A Psychological Research That Helped Change the Field for Good.* New Delhi, India: General Press, 2022.

Mccrea, Peps. *Memorable Teaching: Leveraging Memory to Build Deep and Durable Learning in the Classroom.* Woodbridge, Suffolk: John Catt Educational, 2019.

Moorman, Chick. *Talk Sense to Yourself: The language of Personal Power.* Portage, MI: Personal Power Press, 1985.

Pondiscio, Robert. *How the Other Half Learns: Equality, Excellence, and the Battle Over School Choice.* New York: Avery, 2020.

Sherrington, Tom, and Oliver Caviglioli. *Teaching Walkthrus: Five-Step Guides to Instructional Coaching.* Melton, Woodbridge: John Catt Educational Ltd, 2022.

Skinner, B. F. *About Behaviorism.* New York: Knopf, 1974.

Sullivan, Dan, and Benjamin Hardy. *10x is Easier Than 2x: How World-Class Entrepreneurs Achieve More by Doing Less.* Carlsbad, CA: Hay House Business, 2023.

Sunstein, Cass R. *Conformity: The Power of Social Influences.* New York: New York University Press, 2021.

Suriadi, Ahmad. "Translation Strategies of English Idiomatic Expression in Sherlock Holmes "The Six Thatcher" Film." 2018, https://core.ac.uk/download/326751354.pdf.

Taylor, Charlie. *Divas and Door Slammers*. London: Vermilion, 2010.

Urban, Hal. *Life's Greatest Lessons: 20 Things That Matter*. New York: Simon & Schuster, 2005.

Usher, Marius, Zohar Russo, Mark Weyers, Ran Brauner, and Dan Zakay. "The Impact of the Mode of Thought in Complex Decisions: Intuitive Decisions are Better." *Frontiers in psychology* 2 (2011): 37.

Waitzkin, Josh. *The Art of Learning: A Journey in the Pursuit of Excellence*. London: Simon & Schuster, 2008.

Wiliam, Dylan. *Creating the Schools Our Children Need: Why What We're Doing Now Won't Help Much (and what we can do instead)*. West Palm Beach, FL: Learning Sciences International, 2018.

Wiliam, Dylan. *Leadership for Teacher Learning*. Morrabbin, Vic., 20

Willingham, Daniel T. *When Can You Trust the Experts? How to Tell Good Science From Bad in Education*. San Francisco: Jossey-Bass, a Wiley imprint, 2012.

Willingham, Daniel T. *Why Don't Students Like School?: A Cognitive Scientist Answers Questions About How The Mind Works and What it Means for the Classroom*. Hoboken, NJ: Jossey-Bass, 2021.

Yen, C., Lin, C., & Chiang, M. (2023). *Exploring the Frontiers of Neuroimaging: A Review of Recent Advances in Understanding Brain Functioning and Disorders*. Life, 13(7), 1472. https://doi.org/10.3390/life13071472

Zull, James E. *The Art of Changing the Brain: Enriching Teaching by Exploring the Biology of Learning*. Sterling, VA: Stylus, 2002.

Check Out Our FREE

1-Minute Tips, Activities, and Articles

AND

Subscribe to get our

#1 REQUESTED GUIDE as a FREE BONUS:

FROM APATHY TO AMBITION

The Top 3 Brain Secrets to

Motivate Lazy Learners!

Join Us Now at:

EngagingEducatorsToday.com

Made in the USA
Monee, IL
16 May 2024

58514828R00085